COMMUNICATING ON THE PLAYING FIELD

JOSEF SOLC

Communicating on the Playing Field
By Josef Solc

Printed in the United States of America

ISBN 978-1-60791-763-2

www.xulonpress.com

ENDORSEMENTS

Arnold Toynbee long ago focused attention on the fact that historically the preoccupation with spectator sports was less than healthy for the social order. However, in America world-wide participation in sports is here to stay and any adverse affects on the social order can be somewhat ameliorated by the perceptive proposal provided in this book *Communicating on the Playing Field by Dr. Josef Solc,* Professor of Evangelism and Missions at Southeastern Baptist Theological Seminary in Wake Forest, NC. Dr. Solc himself, formerly the best known men's tennis champion in Czechoslovakia, brings together an experiential grasp of the "playing field" with a thorough understanding of what one must do in order to share effectively the message of Christ. Churches increasingly find that athletics in a wide variety of presentation provides one of the finest opportunities to present Christ to men and boys, or to young people and adults, who often otherwise would not pause long enough to listen. This is a biblically based approach to evangelism in the arena of sports. Every leader interested in reaching the maximum number of people for Christ should read this book.

Paige Patterson
President, Southwestern Baptist Theological Seminary, Fort Worth, Texas

Dr. Solc is no mere academic in the sphere of sports evangelism. As an avid and professional athlete, he has embodied the ministry ethic of sports evangelism in his life. He is convinced that Christ wants the Truth of the gospel proclaimed in every area of life. The sports arena is no exception. As a pastor he has had also a dynamic sports ministry outreach as part of his church program. It merited positive coverage on the sports pages of a key Fort Worth newspaper. During his career he has been active in sponsoring sports evangelism nationally and internationally. But for success in this program Solc recognized the need for strategic vision, organization and perseverance in the task. Here he presents the challenge... read it, enjoy it and be energized to use the sports evangelism ministry for the extension of God's Kingdom.

Jack Roeda
Latin American coordinator for the Spanish Radio-TV programming of the Back to God Hour

Sports evangelism is the easiest, least expensive and most effective way to reach a lost culture. In *Communicating on the Playing Field,* Dr. Josef Solc has presented the theological and practical implications of sports evangelism in such a way that even the most nominal sports enthusiast will be moved to embrace the methods. This book will help those who want to be true evangelism strategists see that sports is the language that can break every cultural barrier.

Rev. Victor Lee
Sports Evangelism Consultant,
North American Mission Board,
Columnist, Sports Spectrum magazine

Communicating on the Playing Field seeks to show how we can use sports for the proclamation of the gospel of Jesus Christ. You will especially appreciate the personal stories shared in this book and the practical wisdom shared in the final chapter.

Daniel Akin
President, Southeastern Baptist Theological Seminary,
Wake Forest, North Carolina

DEDICATION

I dedicate this book to my dearest wife Joy, who encouraged me on many occasions to complete the manuscript, and to my three wonderful children, Joy, Maria, and Josef, who have already put into practice the ministry of sports evangelism.

I also dedicate this book to my parents in law, Jack and Rachel Roeda, who read my manuscript and affirmed my effort in constructive ways.

CONTENTS

INTRODUCTION

The popularity of sports in America and in the rest of the world is undeniable. Sports provide a way of communication that the people of the world readily understand and are willing to participate in. This communication is available in spite of cultural, social, political, religious, and linguistic barriers. A man from America, capable of playing soccer, can enjoy kicking the ball with Brazilians on the streets of Rio de Janeiro as much as he can engage in the same activity with soccer players in a stadium in Frankfurt, Germany. Sports have their own universal language.

Sports can open the door to individual encounters that are so important for Christians who desire to share their faith. These encounters are limitless. Two skiers can meet on the chair lift and will spend the rest of the day skiing together and enjoying the day of healthy activity. A group of ice hockey players can play for fun and after the game will go to relax over a meal in the restaurant with an opportunity to discuss their scoring chances and future plans. And who would challenge the fact that some people play golf just to socialize with others in a beautiful environment of a well groomed golf course. These examples could go on and on, but it will suffice to say that in a world that is as impersonal as ours, sports bring individuals together.

There is, however, another interesting thing about sports. Those who do not play sports are not left out from meeting others. Spectators can meet with like-minded people as they watch their favorite team. This might not work if they are seated next to fans cheering for the visiting team, but one never knows! It might be a pleasant experience even under those circumstances. Spectators love to see a stadium filled with excited fans.

Sports can also engage nearly all nations of the world in a unified sports experience we call the Olympic Games. The world stops for two weeks every other year when all sports minded people, about 95% of all people living in our world, are interested in the results of worldwide competition. They cheer the athletes from their respective countries and are elated when they win medals, or they are saddened when they lose. Yet, in spite of the joy of victory and the despair of defeat, the world gets together over and over again to compete in sports. This achievement is unparalleled in relationships among people and nations. In China, during the 2008 Olympic Games, 205 nations participated in celebrating "one world, one dream". Jacques Rogge, the president of IOC, praised the athletes of the world during his closing address, "You have shown us the unifying power of sport. The Olympic spirit lives in the warm embrace of competitive rivals from nations in conflict."

There is a yearning in the hearts of Christians to bring the world together through faith in Jesus Christ who is the Savior of the world and who is capable of improving the life here on earth and who offers eternal life with him in heaven. But the truth of the matter is that some nations will not even allow Christians to present the Good News in their lands. This is also true about secular individuals who reject or are not interested in anything Christians do or say. This fact looms as an enormous obstacle for the evangelization of the world. Our traditional ways of doing evangelism have not been producing desired results; therefore, we must discover ways that would open the doors for renewed efforts to reach all nations.

One way to influence people around us is through sports. Many people either play sports or love to watch them.

Christians can join them in a non-threatening way and can establish relationships with them. An invitation to attend a church service may go unheeded, but an offer to play sports will be joyfully accepted. Strangers will speak the same language. Strangers can engage in an activity that is good for their physical and emotional wellness. Before long they are not strangers, but friends. The sport they love will provide a common ground that will facilitate opportunities that did not even exist before.

As a pastor, I did my share of outreach in the community around my church. I knocked on thousands of doors, but only seldom I felt welcome. As if I were an intruder who encroached on people's time they didn't want to give. I was convinced of the urgency to proclaim the gospel and at the same time I questioned the way I went about it. Then our church moved to a new location when we bought a Racquet Club with 12 tennis courts, a large swimming pool, a soccer field, and a clubhouse. We invited the people of our community to enjoy our facility. We organized tennis clinics and offered swimming lessons. Non-Christians who would have never thought of rubbing shoulders with Christians before, participated gladly. I remember especially one tennis player who loved to play tennis but showed no interest in spiritual things. First, I just played tennis with him, but later on he started asking questions about things concerning God and heaven. I was able to answer some questions he had, and then he was willing to hear more. Eventually, I presented the gospel to him and he became a Christian. I baptized him and taught him in a Sunday School class while we continued playing tennis as well. A similar scenario happened with others who came to swim or to play tennis.

My experiences as an athlete and pastor have convinced me that Christians have not even begun to uncover the potential of sports evangelism. There have been some bright but sporadic attempts to use this method of evangelism. It is my hope that this book will encourage and equip multitudes of sports evangelists who will witness effectively to sports people.

CHAPTER ONE

CHRISTIANITY AND SPORTS

Emil Zatopek was one of the greatest long-distance runners ever to run in the Olympic Games. In 1952 he won three races at the Helsinki Olympic Games. No runner could outrun him in the 5,000m, 10,000m, and in his first-ever marathon race. He became a Czech national hero who was known throughout the world thanks to his athletic achievements. But there was more to Zatopek than running. He was a committed Christian who was not afraid to profess his faith in spite of living in an atheistic society. When he dared to protest against the Russian invasion into Czechoslovakia in August of 1968, he was degraded from his rank in the army to being a factory worker. Yet, Zatopek knew how to overcome persecution because of his inner strength coming from his relationship with Christ. He said, "All the effort in the battle for life would have no purpose if I did not have Christ before my eyes. It amazes me that God showed us His love by sending Jesus Christ to the world. His sacrifice cleanses us daily from the dirt of sin. This faith in Christ provides the strength to live. First of all, people must expose themselves to the light of the Gospel so that it may radiate through them. After He lights up the path of our lives, we can begin to walk along it."[1] This was a remarkable example of a courageous combination of a Christian witness and sports in a time and place where such a combination was not acceptable. If Zatopek were not a world famous athlete, he would have been removed from the public eye immediately; however, even he had to pay for his faith. In 1968, after his criticism of the Russian invasion, Zatopek was dismissed from the Czech army and became an anonymous person in his home country.

Christian athletes in America and the Western world do not face such problems, but their expressions of faith are not readily accepted either. Should Christianity be kept only among the four walls of church buildings and not to intrude into the sports arenas? Should this marriage of Christianity and sports be avoided? Do they belong to completely different spheres of life? Zatopek would argue that Christianity and sports go together. Top athletes of the world can perform better as they are strengthened by their faith in Christ and as they have purpose for life that goes beyond the temporal scene of winning races and games.

This chapter will deal with the relationship of Christianity and sports in our world that is definitely sports oriented. It is in this kind of a world that Christians need to determine how to relate to it so that the Christian witness would not be pushed out of the arena that boasts of nearly total participation among all nations of the world. Since the commandment of Christ is to go unto all nations, sport is the natural activity that relates to people who do not see their need of Christ, but who enjoy playing or watching sports.

HISTORICAL BACKGROUND OF SPORTS

1. Engaging in play

The starting point for the history of sports is linked with play. People are naturally playful. They desire to get above the routine tasks of each day by engaging in play. Children are very creative when it comes to play. They use ordinary objects as they playfully entertain themselves. Nobody has to teach them how to invent their own games. They even play with their invisible friends and get satisfaction from that alternative to just being alone. Moltmann suggests that even God engaged in play during creation, "The world as free creation cannot be a necessary unfolding of God nor an emanation of his being from his divine fullness. God is free. But he does not act capriciously. When he creates something that is not god but also not nothing, then this must have its ground not in itself but in God's good will or pleasure. Hence the creation is God's play, a play of his goodness and inscrutable wisdom. It is the realm in which God displays his glory."[2] If we admit that Moltmann is right, then we can go on to assert that human play is also not necessary, but is practiced by all people for pure enjoyment. However, there is a difference between God and us because God is not limited in his options. He can create out of nothing and so his playing has no limits. On the other hand, people can merely play with that which is available to them. Yet, they exercise freedom as they determine what forms of play give them the greatest pleasure. Some like to play cards, and others would rather play with their pets. Here lies the enjoyment of play. We immerse ourselves in playing knowing that our freedom will not cease. We thus continue trying to explore the adventures of play.

Allen Guttmann defines play as, "any nonutilitarian physical or intellectual activity pursued for its own sake."[3]

There is no real purpose in play. There is no real goal to be achieved. There is no time limit or specified way to do things. Play happens spontaneously, just for the fun of it.

Play enlarges life beyond doing the necessary, or being just useful to families and society. The Westminster Catechism answers the question, "What is the chief end of man?" It is "to glorify God and to enjoy Him forever." In being playful we join God in this world of joy and sorrow, victory and defeat, health and illness, and rejoicing and suffering. All these contrasts of human existence can be handled from the perspective of occasional play that reminds us of our freedom to glorify God and to enjoy Him forever. This approach to life is superior to totalitarian ideologies that make promises of liberation, but at the same time engage in exploitation that has nearly no room for play. All that is required is usefulness and service to the state. Control is cherished above freedom.

The spirit of play is in its adventure. When people encounter a new situation and are willing to risk the unknown, they rejoice in the exhilaration of the newly found pleasure. No wonder that play has been with us from the beginning of mankind. The adventurer repeats freely his playful experiences because they are ever new. It is never the same when he is risking playing without any guarantee of a positive outcome. He is there facing danger in hope of a striking experience.

A child might venture out on his own exploring nature and forgetting that he might get lost. An adult might jump from an airplane trusting his parachute to bring him safely to the ground. That jump is worth it because of the beauty of being part of the skyline and because of the flight towards the earth that cannot be experienced in any other way. Even though success is not always achieved while people play, the adventure itself is overwhelming.

The desire to play is the strongest in our childhood. Children like to explore in a playful manner. Everything seems to be an adventure; a bubble escaping the mouth, a ball rolling down the street, food thrown purposefully from the high chair to the ground, or tickling the toes of someone who fell asleep. Play gets more complex when children go to school. They do not find simple things amusing. Here we have to make a distinction between spontaneous play and regulated play. When we introduce rules to play, we move to playing games. We play games for a simple enjoyment. Games can be nonutilitarian as well and so remain within the realm of play. Examples of such games are "playing doctor," monopoly, and leapfrog. But we can also include the game of basketball when nobody keeps the score, but everybody is running, scoring, and having fun. We depend on games that others structure for us. Video games would not be selling millions of copies each year without our proclivity to engage in play that seems real.

It is a fact of life that mature adults lose some of the wonder and desire for adventure. Then they are willing to observe others who are playing. That is the reason why they go to sports events, or just sit at home and watch their favorite teams on TV. While watching, they hope against hope that they would be on the field straining, risking, and winning just like the athletes in the stadium or on the screen. Yet, it is possible for adults to experience profound adventure, if they are willing to do what they did as children, namely, to be open to chance, risk, and danger again. Moses exemplified this attitude in his eighties when he saw the burning bush. He did not just pass by. Or he did not try to put the fire out. He stopped, enjoyed the bright fire, took his shoes off, and encountered God all alone in God's nature. The place was no longer the same. Moses was transformed by this experience of playful rejoicing of something profoundly different. He did not miss his chance.

2. Playing sports.

The close connection of play, games, and sports is evident. As play progressed, there was a need for structure and rules that would control games. When more people played together, they wanted to outdo each other. Competition resulted and sports were born. Now there was a possibility to know if one lost or won. Risk became clearly defined and danger increased. Ballantine defines sport as, "a particular way of using leisure time in a combination of physical and mental skills in a competitive way leading to a set of aims/goals by which the contest is won or lost."[4] Sports were no longer mere play. Sports challenged individuals to compete against each other, in contrast to play that could be individual and non competitive. Due to the competitive nature of sports, devotion to excellence and winning entered the scene and resembled the commitment to religion.

Sport and religion have existed together from the ancient times. The Egyptians worshipped goddess Sehet as the goddess of sport. The Greeks held the Ancient Olympic Games for the first time on Olympia in 776 BC known for its magnificent temple to Zeus. They honored Zeus through the Olympic Games every four years. These games were so important that the Greeks counted their time in Olympiads rather than by years. Olympia became the very center of the religious, sporting, and cultural events in Ancient Greece. Those who participated in the Olympic Games did so as unto their gods. The religious element could not be denied. Since these events became a celebration of pagan religiosity, the emperor Theodosius ordered the end of the Olympic Games in 393 AD. He considered the games to be in competition with Christianity. He would not tolerate other activities that would challenge the supreme position of the official Christian religion of the Roman Empire.

Here was the very first conflict between sports and Christianity. Theodosius' defense of Christianity was alien to the approach the apostle Paul would have taken. Paul had no problem comparing athletes to Christians since both were examples of striving to win a race. He wrote, "Do you not know that in a race all the runners run, but only one gets the prize? Run in such a way as to get the prize. Everyone who competes in the games, goes into strict training. They do it to get a crown that will not last; but we do it to get a crown that will last forever. Therefore do not run like a man running aimlessly; I do not fight like a man beating the air. No, I beat my body and make it my slave so that after I have preached to others, I myself will not be disqualified for the prize." (I Cor. 9:24-27) Paul probably watched the Isthmus games in Corinth while he stayed there and was sufficiently impressed with those athletes to make comparisons between their effort and that of Christians. He realized that in order to reach the masses of the first century, he could not overlook the appeal of sports. He familiarized himself with sports and contextualized his approach so that nobody would be left out. He wanted to become "all things to all men" I Cor. 9:22.

Early Christian leaders did not follow Paul's example. They did not catch up with the masses as is evident in Chrysostom's statement, "If you ask Christians who is Amos or Obadiah, how many apostles there were or prophets, they stand mute; but if you ask them about the horses or drivers they answer with more solemnity than rhetors."[5] Is it possible that the gladiatorial contests where Christians were the victims became the source of apprehension for games and sports even later on? No matter how much the Christian leaders disliked sports, they did not prevent Christians from being enchanted by them. And when the idolatrous elements of sports were removed, the tide could not be stopped. When Christianity became the empire's religion, Christians participated in their culture and embraced sports, but they did not forget to be constantly critical of possible abuses connected with sports. Their involvement was not overwhelming because of the lack of leisure time. People in general did not have much time left after working each day to provide for the basic necessities of life. The military provided more leisure for soldiers in time of peace to engage in sports like fencing, and archery. These sports became part of festivities enjoyed by many spectators.

Moving on to the Reformation period, some reduction of the Roman Catholic influence opened the door to secularization and more activity in sports. The Puritans objected to playing sports on Sundays in spite of the permission spelled out in The Book of Sports in 1617 that allowed games to be played after worship services. This decision only increased the friction between sports and Christianity. Sports then flourished on their own offering a new variety of sports such as boxing, soccer, and cricket. But it was not until the Industrial Revolution that sports grew in numbers and that spectators were willing and capable to pay for watching their favorite teams.

The church tried to regain its position in the progressively secularized world. The eighteenth and the nineteenth century's revivals both in England and America propelled the church on the stage of the cultural environment that included sports. Some Christians seized this opportunity to reconsider the relationship between Christianity and sports. They introduced sports into Christian schools as part of a permanent curriculum and promoted sports as preparation for life.

They believed that sports would enhance discipline, teamwork, courage, and determination. The positive outcome of this approach resulted in graduates who lived the Christian principles at home and on the foreign mission field. They showed Christian perseverance and skills that made a difference in the world.

The modern world had to wait till the 19th century to rediscover the Olympic Games through the excavations done by Germans in Olympia. Pierre de Coubertin (1863-1937) wanted to go beyond the excavations and recreate the splendor of Olympia by reviving the ancient Olympic Games. He succeeded in his effort when the first Olympic games of the modern time were held in Athens in 1896. He also preserved the close connection between sports and cultural events as he enabled people of many cultures to come together to celebrate not only their athletic achievements, but also their different cultural expressions. Pierre de Coubertin spoke about the religion of the Olympic athletes. Later on Carl Diem broadened the religious vocabulary when in Berlin Olympic Games in 1936 he introduced the Olympic hymn, the Olympic flag, and established a festive ceremony that took on religious dimensions.

The next period of significant progress in sports relating to Christianity was "muscular Christianity". The term appeared first in a review of Charles Kingsley's book *Two Years Ago* in the February 21, 1857 issue of Saturday Review. Thomas Hughes, a personal friend of Kingsley, developed the concept of "muscular Christianity" by stressing traits of manliness, morality, and patriotism. He compared muscular Christians in 1860 with "musclemen" in his book *Tom Brown at Oxford*. He wrote, "The only point in common between the two being, that both hold it to be a good thing to have strong and well-exercised bodies.... Here all likeness ends...The least of the muscular Christians has hold of the old chivalrous and Christian belief, that a man's body is given to be trained and brought into subjection, and then used for the protection of the weak, the advancement of all righteous causes, and the subduing of the earth which God has given to the children of men."[6] Kingsley and Hughes provided impetus for other scholars such as Gerald Redmont, Peter McIntosh, Andrew Miracle, Roger Rees, and Michael Oriard, to pursue the theme of muscular Christianity. Their definitions varied but the four main characteristics could be summed up as "manliness, health, morality, and patriotism."[7] This core ideology was not always interpreted unanimously. It meant different things to different evangelical Christians like Amos Alfonso Stagg, Dwight L. Moody, Charles T. Studd, and Luther Gulick. These small variations did not keep them, however, from affecting significantly the relationship of sports and Christianity within the larger context of society.

Here we have to make a point that could be easily overlooked. Muscular Christianity did not originate in a vacuum. There were societal changes in progress that could have been ignored by Christians and not used for affecting the society. First, industrialization opened the door for new means of production and consumption. More leisure time resulted for workers in major cities where teams found fans to support professional sports. Second, fourteen million immigrants came to the United States between 1865 and 1900. The increase in population meant more spectators in stadiums and more revenues for sports. Third, educational facilities were built and students participated in competitive sports. Fourth, with increased productivity, there was more money for capital development. Owners and managers of teams provided structures for building sports facilities and forming leagues that would declare through elimination the ultimate winner. All of this could have gone unnoticed by Christians. They could have gone on doing church in their sanctuaries as it is done quite often even in our day. But the proponents of muscular Christianity saw a unique opportunity to be right in the midst of these major changes. They knew they could serve as catalysts in this new era.

A contextualized Christian movement was born first in England and later on in America. But this linkage was not to continue without any problems. There were periods of engagement and disengagement between muscular Christianity and sports due to strong critical forces in the evangelical community. Billy Sunday, an exceptional baseball player, who became a famous evangelist, saw the benefits of linking Christianity with sports. He used baseball illustrations in his preaching, won many people for Christ, but turned against sports later in his ministry. The next great evangelist, Billy Graham, was instrumental in a new engagement with sports by asking major professional athletes to testify about their faith during his crusades. He also held his meetings in the biggest stadiums throughout the world. People came to hear him and felt at home in familiar surroundings. This helped him to gain important credibility among nominal Christians and sports minded people in general. Graham reintroduced the church and sports to each other and so overcame, to a certain degree, the cultural isolation of Christianity in an increasingly secular society of the twentieth century.

Para church organizations discovered the field of sports as a new way to connect with the unchurched. New institutions came into existence such as Sports Ambassadors, the Fellowship of Christian Athletes, Athletes in Action, the

International Sports Coalition, and Sports Outreach America. Since these organizations were created for the purpose of engaging Christians in the field of sports, the continuation of Christian ministries among sports minded people was not only guaranteed, but also mushroomed. Sports, education, and the evangelical churches invented networks and programs of mutual cooperation that flourished and are with us in the 21st century. The question remains whether this progress will continue or not. To decide on the proper response, we will explore the similarities of Christianity and sports first.

SIMILARITIES BETWEEN CHRISTIANITY AND SPORTS

At first sight, the linkage of Christianity and sports seems unlikely. One can argue that they belong to different areas of life and that any similarities are merely artificial. But there is another possible approach to this dilemma. Christianity and sports can be identified as religions. Sociologists define religion as "a socially shared set of beliefs and rituals focused on the ultimate concerns of human existence: birth, life, suffering, illness, tragedy, injustice, and death. Religious beliefs and rituals consist of meanings and cultural practices that are special because people connect them with a sacred and supernatural realm and base these connections primarily on faith, the foundation for most religions and religious beliefs."[8] All people do not clearly or identically define the sacred and the supernatural realm. Some believe in the only true God, and others prefer to believe in many gods whom they can manipulate and use for their personal advantage. But the final result is that these systems of meaning influence the organization of social life. Whether it is Christianity or sports, they become a part of the cultural landscape. They share the same culture as they affect it and develop alongside it. An analysis of this process might be more helpful to Christianity than sports because sports have outpaced Christianity in getting the attention of the secularized population. Bob Briner was alarmed by this progression when he said, "Instead of hanging around the fringes of our culture, we need to be right smack dab in the middle of it."[9] A list of similarities between Christianity and sports will alert us to ways that Christians have had at their disposal but are not using them sufficiently.

- A good starting point is in the universal appeal. Christianity is the most widespread religion in our world and sports are played in every country of the world. Sports are even considered to be the universal language that is available for the rich and poor, the educated and uneducated, all races, the great and not so great athletes, and finally even the spectators. Christianity and sports share the world stage and lately sports get more attention, participation, and time.

- A more specific similarity lies in the places and buildings where Christianity and sports happen. In the past, Christian buildings were the focal points of villages, towns, and big cities. Large cathedrals defined the horizon of wealthy cities indicating the importance of worshipping God. Inside were statues of the crucified Christ and the saints who tried to imitate Him. The walls depicted sacred events painted by the most famous artists of each era. The beauty of these cathedrals is appreciated and admired even now, but they are no longer the focal points of the cultural life in the postmodern world. Owners and managers of sports teams realized their need for spacious and well-designed stadiums. With the help of local city governments, they are building stadiums that are much bigger, but not more beautiful, than the biggest cathedrals. These stadiums provide for the worship of super stars whose names, pictures, and jerseys proudly decorate sports sanctuaries.

- A closely related similarity are the precise times and schedules of events. The church year includes the same events every year. Pastors and priests develop sermons that relate to the birth, death, and the resurrection of Christ. They gather their congregations and deliver their sermons at a specific time on Sunday, usually at 11:00 am. Lately the days and times for worship services have been questioned and sometimes changed, but they still happen at certain times. In sports, games are scheduled for the whole season. Times and days are precisely determined so that nobody would have to guess when to see the desired event. Next to regularly scheduled events, there are those special times when the best play each other to declare the champion of the world. Here again sports are ahead of Christianity. It seems that the world stops every two years to watch the Olympic Games. These games bring the world together in a euphoric worship of human achievement and solidarity. There are other events that bring about religious excitement in the hearts of athletes and spectators like the World Cup in soccer, the Super Bowl in football, Wimbledon's two weeks battle for the tennis crown, and the playoffs in baseball and basketball.

- Sports and Christianity have rituals. Sports are based on secular faith and Christianity on sacred faith. Any faith demands order and rules that give religion its form. Sports have national anthems for events of national proportions, exchanging of flags, introduction of players, referees keeping the fair play, halftime shows to keep spectators entertained at all times, cheerleaders making sure that the spectators get into the game as much as possible insuring the support of the home team, and finally hand shaking and congratulating the winners. Christianity has ceremonial rituals that perpetuate the most important things of relating to God and one another. Jesus Christ instituted two sacraments, namely, baptism and the Lord's Supper. Christians do not observe both of them every Sunday, but they are part of the overall life of every local church. Other rituals are not as significant, but are practiced by Christians freely such as singing old hymns and praise songs, prayers for different occasions, giving money to the church, responsive reading from the Bible, sermons, the joining of hands to express the value of fellowship before God, pronouncing a benediction, and meeting the pastor on the way out of the sanctuary.

- Both Christianity and sports emphasize the need for improvement of body, mind, and spirit. Christianity has a goal that is perfection. Christ said, "Be perfect, therefore, as your heavenly Father is perfect" (Matt. 5:48 NIV). The context of this passage reveals the need for perfect love, which we cannot attain in this life. Yet it does not say that we can do away with this command. We must keep on reaching toward that goal. The process of sanctification must go on till we are more and more like Christ. Puritans concentrated their efforts on the spiritual and mental improvements at the expense of bodily exercise and development. Writers like Dallas Willard and Richard Foster corrected this omission by stressing the fact that there is little spiritual progress possible in the life of a Christian whose body is sickly. Sports, on the other hand, do neglect the spiritual side necessary for the overall improvement of athletes. Sports demand nearly perfect bodies for breaking world records and winning world championships. For that purpose, athletes are willing to enhance their performance by drugs that eventually cause malfunction in their bodies. Here Christianity can positively influence sports by teaching athletes about the spiritual dimension of competition that is guided by God given moral principles.

- Commitment is the next similarity. Christianity demands total commitment to Christ and His teachings. “Then Jesus said to his disciples, ‘If anyone would come after me, he must deny himself and take up his cross and follow me. For whoever wants to save his life will lose it, but whoever will lose his life for me will find it” (Matthew 16: 24-25 NIV). There is no greater commitment than to be willing to die for someone else in order to propagate his teachings. And that is exactly what Christ asks for in this statement. Nothing less will do. Many Christians either do not know about this demand, or are not quite ready to live that way. But history teaches us that Christian martyrs were willing to bring this ultimate sacrifice because of their total commitment to Christ.

The great athlete shows a similar attitude. His life is completely focused on his training and involvement in the sport where he wants to prove his superiority and world domination. He pays no attention to distractions of the every day life because he knows that without a single-minded devotion and commitment to his sport there is no ultimate victory. No wonder Paul uses athletes as examples to Christians on how to live the Christian life. "Everyone who competes in the games goes into strict training. They do it to get a crown that does not last; but we do it to get a crown that will last forever" (I Cor. 9:25 NIV). In II Timothy 2:5 Paul writes, "Similarly, if anyone competes as an athlete, he does not receive the victor's crown unless he competes according to the rules." Commitment within the rules is the ideal. Christianity has a great opportunity in this area to correct some of the aberrations in modern sports.

- Large institutions are vital for sports and Christianity. The church grew rapidly in the first century, but it was not until Christianity became the state religion of the Roman Empire in 375 AD that the hierarchical system of authority developed and became a powerful institution influencing not only the church but the world as well. Squabbles over who should run the church resulted in a major division of the West and the East. Tradition and false teachings gained acceptance among many Christians and the church had to correct its teachings through a major reforming effort led by Martin Luther in Germany. With the Reformation in place, new denominations formed and the Roman Catholic Church had to accept competition from Protestant churches. Catholics have a pope, cardinals, bishops, and priests. Protestants have presidents, chairmen, pastors, elders, and lay leaders. At the present moment, there is no institution in place that would truly unite and guide all Christians. Sports had to wait much longer for an effort to create national sports organizations. England led the way in the middle of the nineteenth century. International organizations followed and the crowning result of this development was the birth of the International Olympic Committee in 1894.

Many nations saw the need to establish a governmental sports bureaucracy to control and regulate national sports through a central institution. A major sports powerhouse, the United States of America, is the exception, as if Americans did not need a central agency. The only time sports administrators try to cooperate in their efforts is once in two years in order to create an American Olympic team representing the United States on the world forum. Hopefully, the American individualistic spirit will give in to the cooperative effort to facilitate a network that would provide for the best sports competition in all states and throughout the world. It is interesting to note that even the church denominations in America do not have a nation wide church organization that would be acceptable to all Christians. The World Council of Churches is looked upon with suspicion by conservative denominations such as the Southern Baptist Convention, the largest Protestant denomination in America. Since there is nothing comparable to the Olympic Games in Christianity, there is just about no constructive effort made to create a world wide event that would bring all churches together for a worshipful celebration where the ritual would be accepted and enjoyed by all.

- Our world demands records and statistics. Christianity and sports keep records. The Book of Acts records the beginning of the church by presenting the progression of growth. Acts 1:15 speaks about 120 Christians forming the first group of Christians. Then in Acts 2:41 3,000 people were added through baptism. Acts 4:4 states that the number grew to 5, 000. Luke made sure that the numbers would tell the story, but later on in Acts 5:14 he was satisfied by simply giving a general information, "Nevertheless, more and more men and women believed in the Lord and were added to their number." Churches, denominations, and conventions produce numbers each year about their members who are resident and non-resident, how many people were baptized, how many people were added and how many lost, how much money members gave, how many churches were started and how many closed their doors, and how many missionaries are on the foreign mission field. Sports records are much more complicated and numerous. Columns after columns are printed every day in local newspapers. But that is not enough. There are specialized magazines that print statistics for individual sports and their athletes. Summaries of each year are recorded for those who might miss some of the information throughout the year. Record keeping is a trait of the modern age.

The Greeks did not write down their measurable records for us. They enjoyed those who won. The winner received the crown. He was the best. Nothing else mattered. Our preoccupation with numbers and time forced athletes to compete not only against each other, but also against time and meters. The pressure was increased, and improvement was expected. Athletes who reached the championship level acquired a special status in the eyes of their fans. Another similarity came into existence.

- Christianity and sports have their heroes, legends, and saints. The Roman Catholic Church continues selecting individual Christians to sainthood and encourages their members to pray to them. This is a form of idolatry rejected by Protestants, but putting famous preachers, missionaries, and faith healers on a pedestal comes close to what is in principle denied. There is no hesitation among fans to call their favorite athletes stars, and super stars. They are being worshiped and celebrated as more than human. Reporters tell embellished stories about them and so create the aura of supremacy at least in sports. Any worship of human beings presents wide-ranging problems in morality, honesty, faithfulness, and decency. A winning athlete is not always winning in life; therefore, fans should exercise caution in making them examples and heroes. But our world does not pay attention to this warning. Spectators want these heroes and will overlook and forgive most mistakes and crimes committed by the super stars. Inductions into halls of fame flourish and are perpetuated by sports organizations.

Christianity is not quite blameless, but could address and correct some of the problems associated with a hero worship. A clear warning should sound based on Exodus 20:3-5, "You shall have no other gods before me. You shall not make for yourself an idol in the form of anything in heaven above or on the earth beneath or in the waters below. You shall not bow down to them or worship them; for I, the Lord your God, am a jealous God."

- Heroes do not appear without specialization. The time is long gone when players could excel in two major sports. There are only a handful of athletes who are capable of playing two sports on the highest professional level. The rule is that the very best play only one sport. Christianity bought into this system by creating the clergy and the lay people. Those who accept an office in the church are educated and qualified to preach, teach, administer, counsel, lead the music, train youth, and provide for many activities. The lay people are overlooked and degraded to jobs that are not as 'important'. This kind of segregation prevents the church from involving more and more people in the life of a local church. The end result is that the majority of Christians are spectators, just like fans in sports, and will never know the beauty and satisfaction of being in the very center of serving their God. This specialization is bringing illusory comfort to those who want to sit on the sidelines; however, this is not the Christian life that Christ envisioned for all Christians when he said, "All authority in heaven and on earth has been given to me. Therefore go make disciples of all nations, baptizing them in the name of the Father and of the Son and of the Holy

Spirit, and teaching them to obey everything I have commanded you. And surely I am with you always, to the end of the age (Matthew 28:18-20).

Paul issued a similar command in I Timothy 6:12 "Fight the good fight of the faith. Take hold of the eternal life to which you were called in the presence of many witnesses." There is no room for spectators in Christianity. But the influence of sports is changing Christianity. Many Christians are now satisfied when they watch others fighting the good fight of faith. What a loss for them individually and for God's kingdom corporately.

- Sports are also winning in creating more excitement. Fans go to games and matches to enjoy themselves and to let their emotions go. Some of it is programmed with the help of cheerleaders, but most excitement is spontaneous. There is nothing like it when the home team scores a touchdown, or hits a homerun. At that point fans go crazy, are loud, give each other high fives, sing songs, and become extremely excited. The fans of the opposite team are sad, quiet, angry with their team and the referees, and possibly are crying when the game is over. Such a range of emotions is scarcely seen anywhere else. In comparison, Christians are more composed during worship services expressing their emotions through songs, raised hands, shouting amen and hallelujah, and occasionally encouraging their preacher to get with it. Realizing that people have more fun outside the church than inside, rich churches try to supply more excitement through performances of known professional artists, but the smaller congregations are left behind since they do not have the money to pay. In all fairness, Christian excitement must be within the hearts of those who worship God. Producing it by any other means betrays the shallowness of our worship and discipleship. Paul's command "Rejoice in the Lord always" (Philippians 4:4) is a great possibility for all Christians. Can you imagine what would be the excitement of Christians of this caliber when they get together to worship God?

- Purpose is something that both Christianity and sports provide. True Christian life is far ahead of sports in this area. Speaking about purpose must include the reality of life beyond death so that the temporary issue of striving would have an ultimate meaning. The words of Jesus Christ speak clearly, "What will it benefit a man if he gains the whole world yet loses his life? Or what will a man give in exchange for his life? For the Son of Man is going to come with His angels in the glory of His Father, and then He will reward each according to what he has done" (Matthew 16:26-27). Sports provide a definite purpose especially for young people. They can devote themselves fully to training and playing sports to become the best. They give it all they have with the help of their parents who want them to be successful. But what happens to those who do not make it? Or even worse, what happens to those who reach the top and get older? Their bodies no longer function as before and they must retire in their 30s or very few in their early 40s.

No superstar can prepare himself for the end of his career. John Elway expressed his thoughts, "My whole life I had a carrot to chase…for 16 years, winning the Super Bowl was my carrot. Everything revolved around that. All of a sudden there's no carrot anymore, and you start wondering what you're going to do with your life. You play golf or try business stuff, but it's not even close. You end up spinning yourself like a tornado."[10] There is a vacuum in this passage that simply does not go away. It is over. There is no chance to regain the splendor of being the best in the world whether it is Mohamed Ali or Pele. The search for an overarching purpose starts usually for professional athletes when their career is over. Some of them commit their lives to Jesus Christ and later testify about the importance of gaining purpose that is valid beyond this life.

- The final similarity concerns the accusation of Karl Marx that Christianity distracts people from the real issues and problems in life. He was raised in a Jewish Christian family, but rejected Christianity and characterized it as the opiate of the masses of people. He completely overlooked the fact that Christians were not just heavenward oriented. If he studied the overall history of Christian missions, he would have to take his criticism back. Missionaries became educators, medical doctors, agricultural experts, translators of the Bible, humanitarians, and progressive thinkers in primitive cultures. The teachings of Christ benefited humanity for twenty centuries even though there were some aberrations of the application of his truths.

Surprisingly, this criticism is voiced against sports as well. Coakley claims that sports "can distract attention from important social, political, and economic issues and thereby become an 'opiate' of the masses of people in society."[11] This valuation is partly true, but not quite legitimate. People gravitate towards sports because of their tendency to play and to compete. Holding it against them would be making them less than human. There is an essential need to escape the routine things of life, and sports provide that escape which is, however, not quite complete. Since 95% of all people are involved to some extent in sports, if this criticism was correct, important social, political, and economic issues would not be sufficiently addressed. So the reason for the ills of humanity will have to be found somewhere else.

DIFFERENCES BETWEEN CHRISTIANITY AND SPORTS

With so many similarities between Christianity and sports, why should we talk about their differences? We must make this shift because both belong in different spheres of life that we cannot overlook. There are two possible groups of scholars that approach this problem from different perspectives. Essentialists argue that the fundamental character and truth of religion are different from sports because of the profanity of sports. They are afraid that sports will corrupt and secularize Christianity. Functionalists, on the other hand, consider the functional elements that reveal differences of Christianity and sports such as Super Bowl Sunday and Easter Sunday, or Saint Patrick's Cathedral in New York and Yankee Stadium, or singing the national anthem before a hockey game and starting a worship service with a praise song unto God. Both approaches will intermingle in our listing of major differences.

First, there is a difference between the sacred and the profane. The beginning of Christianity is in the special revelation of God through his Son Jesus Christ. Jesus himself describes it in these words, "For God so loved the world that he gave his only begotten son that whosoever believes in him should not perish but have eternal life" (John 3:16). The initiative is of God not men. The continuation of Christianity is in the power of Jesus Christ who said, "I will build my church and the gates of hell will not overcome it" (Matthew 16:18). The future of Christianity is in Christ's promise, "I am with you always, to the end of the age" (Matthew 28:20). Christianity belongs to the sacred realm from first to last. Sports cannot claim anything that would come close to the above affirmations. Even though sports are described as religion-like, they are firmly grounded in the secular realm. Any reminder of the Olympic Games honoring Zeus, will not lift sports up into the sacred realm. The connection to the mythological Greek gods actually imbeds sports even more firmly in the profane concerns of life. The continuation of this practice persists in our postmodern world where people worship superstars as if they were gods.

Second, there is a difference in the transcendent and material outlook on life. Christianity transcends the human condition by looking forward to eternity. This life in not all that Christians will experience. The quality of eternal life begins with the new birth of a man who believes in Christ as Savior and continues improving until arriving into the heavenly home. The intermediate period is filled with many struggles and endeavors, but the victory is guaranteed. Paul states it well, "Who can separate us from the love of Christ? Can affliction or anguish or persecution or famine or nakedness or danger or sword? As it is written: Because of you we are being put to death all day long; we are counted as sheep to be slaughtered. No, in all these things we are more than conquerors through him who loved us" (Romans 8:35-36). Sports have no assurance that transcends the circumstances of an athlete. Sports focus on material issues of temporal significance. Victory is important because it assures benefits like money, fame, awards, commercials, and rewards of many other kinds. And all of this will not happen without the physical effort in training and in competition. Whether the athlete is winning or not, his achievements are limited to this life only.

Third, there is a difference between faith in God and faith in man's capability. There is a definition of faith in Hebrews 11:1, "Now faith is the reality of what is hoped for, the proof of what is not seen." Faith of this quality is the gift of God and Christians live by it. They claim that nothing can separate them from the love of God. They are pilgrims on this earth with a definite goal of being victorious in reaching heaven and spending eternity with their God. Faith is the proof of what they cannot see. Athletes find this faith strange. They depend on their physical abilities, mental prowess, and some help from the coach in order to beat anyone in their way to become the best. And why would it be otherwise? Isn't it evident that they would not have won without their extreme physical and mental effort? Faith in anything or anyone else seems not appropriate. Some superstitions are secretly allowed, but the biblical faith in God does not play a major role in most athletes.

Fourth, there is a difference between rendering a loving service and stressing the individual achievement that demands defeating others. The Christian ideal is that of a servant. Servanthood is the way to greatness. Jesus proclaims it in no uncertain terms, "The greatest among you will be your servant. Whoever exalts himself will be humbled, and whoever humbles himself will be exalted" (Matthew 23:11-12). This teaching is foreign to sports. Athletes and coaches speak about the killer instinct that is necessary to succeed. Opponents must be beaten and titles gained. The only service that will do is serving an ace that nobody can return.

CHRISTIANITY AND SPORTS: INFLUENCE AND BENEFITS

This chapter demonstrated the close relationship of Christianity with sports. The question still remains concerning the interrelationship of these two powerhouses in the present culture. Which is more prominent and why? I will answer this question in concluding remarks. Historically, Christianity was more influential in forming the culture of its environment for many centuries. But things began to change with the dawn of the Enlightenment era. Secular philosophers introduced doubts into the minds of many people by presenting new ideas that rejected the longstanding teachings of Christianity. The secularization process was put in motion. Harvey Cox wrote on this subject in *The Secular City*. He defined secularization as "the delivery of man first from religion and then from metaphysical control over his reason and his language."[12] The French revolution in 1789 provided a definite momentum for this process and the age of modernity was born. It lasted, according to Thomas Oden, until the collapse of communism in 1989 when the Berlin Wall fell. There were at least four motifs in modernity as primary agents of shifting people's thinking from Christianity to secular ideas. These were autonomous individualism, narcissistic hedonism, reductive naturalism, and absolute moral relativism.[13] The autonomous individualism motif is the most important for our evaluation of the secular influence. Friedrich Nietzsche (1844-1900) declared that God was dead and man should assume God's position on earth as a sovereign being. While exercising his will-to-power, man should assert himself in all areas of life. Everything depended on man who was now alone in his universe to forge his future with confidence.

This philosophy of modernity clearly influenced sports. We saw it in the above mentioned differences between Christianity and sports like believing only in man's ability, limiting life to the secular realm, depending only on the material world, and engaging in pleasures offered indiscriminately by wealth and fans. These attitudes brought sports to the forefront of Western cultures and made them at home with people who shared these ideas. Sports grew and became more popular than ever, but Christianity lost much ground.

Is there a lesson here? I believe so. Christians did not immediately recognize the impact of modernity that disrupted much of what was accomplished in sixteen centuries. They did not quite realize that the culture around them was changing drastically. They did not pay enough attention to men like Nietzsche, Freud, Marx, and Darwin who presented ideas that the natural man was embracing without proper analysis. Secular philosophers and scientists appealed to the basic instincts of humankind and succeeded in changing the whole philosophical spectrum of thinking about our universe and society. Marx uncovered his plan when he said, "The philosophers only interpreted the world; however, the point is to change it." He knew his world well enough to turn it upside down. His idea of a classless society was a mere idealistic hope that did not materialize in spite of millions people paying for it with their lives. None of the other modern ideas proved to be realizable or to bring expected satisfaction and lasting fulfillment. So we entered the postmodern period characterized by the despair of finding an objective truth. The idealized hopes of modernity did not come true. People lost a sense of direction and of a bright future ahead of them. But some of the motifs of modernity are surviving especially in sports. So here is the lesson. The world has changed and it will not be the same again. The flux of change is in motion like a runaway train powered by an electrical current. We must figure out how to climb into this train and let our presence known because the people inside of the train face a grave danger, at least from the Christian perspective of God's judgment. There might be many ways how to do it, but I will limit my suggestion to our present topic of the relationship of sports with Christianity. Sports are conquering the western culture and receiving more attention than anything and anybody else. Millions of people would rather go to a football game than to read a scientific book. Millions of parents would rather take their kids to a baseball practice than to have them play a musical instrument. Millions of people, and not just men, would rather read the sport section in the daily newspaper than to digest the editorial on an important issue. Millions of people will pay much money individually to experience the highly emotional atmosphere of car racing on Sunday than to go to church and pay their tithe. They are living up to the post-modern craving for an authentic experience and the church, as a whole, has barely entered the competition. That is the reason why Christians are looked upon as of the past and predominantly insignificant. Yet not all is lost. Christians still gather in their churches. They still try to follow the teachings of Jesus Christ. They just must enter the world as Jesus did. They must and can be the salt and the light of the world.

There is no better place than to join the sport-minded people where they enjoy themselves. Recreational facilities are waiting for us, but I am not talking about family life centers where Christians segregate themselves from the sport culture. Clubs are open for new members. Stadiums are large and can accommodate Christians who will invite their non-Christian friends to watch a game. This can be the most natural way to penetrate the secular culture at home and in the rest of the world.

I visited Bangladesh with the goal of making friends with some people there. During my stops in restaurants, shops, hotels, and universities, I was able to talk to men and women on a superficial level. Then I visited a local tennis club where I introduced myself as a former professional tennis player. An invitation to play with the best player in the club followed immediately. Then I had to play a doubles match with three other players who desired to hit the ball with me. I was exhausted because of the high temperature and humidity there, but those players would not let me leave. They begged me to teach their young people how to play tennis. I did that free for three days. At first I had 15 students, the next day there were 35 youngsters listening to my instruction, and on the third day there were more than 50 beginners eager to learn from me. When the president of the club saw the interest of those young players, he offered me a job as a professional tennis teacher in his club. My students of three days asked me to stay as well. When I said I had to go back to the States to teach in a Christian university, they gave me their pictures and addresses so that I would not forget them. I could not have done anything like this had I not been capable and willing to use sports to befriend those tennis players.

We can benefit from this relationship of Christianity with sports, but we must enter the sports world with determination to build upon our similarities and to uphold our differences. Representing Christ well should convince the postmodern people about the beauty, sacredness, validity, and the possibility of a personal relationship with the Almighty God. He is the only One who can outdo even the greatest human achievement and offer the abundant life. In order to fulfill this task, we must examine the biblical foundations of sports evangelism.

CHAPTER TWO

BIBLICAL FOUNDATIONS FOR SPORTS EVANGELISM

Immediately after my profession of faith in Jesus Christ in 1957, my father told me, "Josef, you should read two chapters in the Bible every day." I agreed to do it because I was hungry to know everything God inspired his people to write down. But I had a big problem. I didn't have my own Bible. Communists established a totalitarian regime in Czechoslovakia and didn't allow Christians to print new Bibles. So my father spent a lot of time going through second hand bookstores in Prague looking for an old and discarded Bible. Finally he succeeded buying a Bible that was falling apart. He asked a friend to bind the Bible in leather and then he gave it to me. I still consider that Bible as a precious gift that I treasure even 50 years later.

I started reading my Bible faithfully. Even though I did not know the terminology, I was doing biblical theology. Slowly but surely I became convinced that I would be able to use sports as a means of sharing the gospel with other athletes and those who wanted to be my friends because of my sports successes. Living in Czechoslovakia presented the danger of persecution, but I witnessed anyway and Jesus protected me from being put into prison. Throughout the years, I was able to witness about my Lord to ice hockey players in a locker room, on the ice when I coached young people, and in banquet halls after important games. I shared the gospel also with tennis players while meeting them repeatedly during professional circuit tournaments and leading Bible studies for those who wanted to know more. Organizing tennis clinics provided many contacts with tennis enthusiasts who were willing to hear the gospel after enjoying the Christian atmosphere on tennis courts. There was no need for me to think about separation of Christianity and sports. I lived among athletes and I counted it a great privilege to represent my Lord and Savior in that international culture. In this way I obeyed the call to go and to make disciples of all nations

There are other examples of people coming to the same conclusion as I did. While studying his Bible, James Naismith became convinced that he could use sports to communicate

Christian values. He loved sports and participated in rugby, gymnastics, and fencing. In 1890 he joined Amos Alonzo Stagg and Luther Gutlick at the YMCA training school in Springfield, Massachusetts. There he came up with the idea of a new game called basketball. Here is what happened,

> One day, before class, Naismith asked James (Pop) Stebbins, the Y's janitor, to find him two large boxes. Instead, Stebbins returned from the storeroom with peach baskets, which Naismith nailed to the balconies at either end of the gym. When the students arrived, Naismith divided them into two groups of nine players. After selecting a center for each team, he tossed up a soccer ball to begin the game. The rules were simple. Players tried to toss the ball into the basket and could bat, pass, and bounce the ball, but couldn't run with it. William R. Chase scored the historic contest's only point on a twenty-foot shot. The ball nestled into the basket, and Stebbins had to climb a ladder to retrieve it.[1]

Naismith realized his goal through teaching basketball in its developmental years. He propagated the importance of keeping balance between exercising the body and acquiring mental skills based on the timeless truths of God. As he coached children, he emphasized discipline, cooperation, team effort, and devotion to God.

Only now we know how helpful Naismith's efforts became in the area of sports evangelism. One man's vision motivated thousands of Christians to get involved in what we know as Upward Basketball. This sports ministry began at a church in Spartanburg, South Carolina in 1986 because of the vision of a recreation minister Caz McCaslin. Upward Basketball is now simply Upward because its ministries include not only basketball, but also cheerleading, flag football and soccer. "Upward is an evangelical sports ministry specifically designed for kindergarten through sixth grade boys and girls that promotes salvation, character, and self-esteem in every child."[2] The growth of this organization is phenomenal. In 1999 there were 76,587 children participating in basketball. In 2005 Upward registered 397,465 children who enjoyed sports and heard the gospel as well. One man's proper biblical understanding of using sports evangelism on the basketball court resulted in thousands of decisions for Christ.

There is nothing in the Bible that would speak directly about sports evangelism. We must be honest about it, but we can find concepts and words that illumine the relationship of sports and Christianity. They coexisted for centuries and were aware of each other; therefore, a study of sports evangelism can be legitimate. To begin with, a general definition of evangelism will be helpful in that it will provide a framework for our thinking. Drummond presents a comprehensive definition, "[Evangelism is] a concerted effort in the power of the Holy Spirit to confront unbelievers with the truth about Jesus Christ and the claims of our Lord (Acts 2:22-23, 31) with a view of leading unbelievers into repentance toward God and faith in our Lord Jesus Christ (Acts 20:21) and thus into the fellowship of His church so they may grow in the Spirit."[3] The initial step in evangelism is to confront unbelievers in the power of the Holy Spirit with the gospel. Here we have to be careful how we understand the word 'to confront'. Confronting someone is not a pleasant experience for either side, but it is essential for the proclamation of the Good News that demands a change in the life of a listener. Repentance and faith must be explained clearly so that the hearers are not misled into some kind of an easy way to heaven. Those who witness about Christ must represent Him in a loving way, but must not lessen or water down the gospel. This we can accomplish by building relationships in the sports arena. Are there any precedents on this subject in the Bible? We will begin by explaining the scope of biblical theology.

Biblical theology limits itself to reading and understanding the Bible. Reading itself is not doing biblical theology. The reader must be a man of faith so that the Holy Spirit would guide him into all truth, "But when he, the Spirit of truth, comes, he will guide you into all truth" (John 16:13). The ideal situation happens when the reader establishes the intention of the biblical writer and interprets the text for his time. There must be a close relationship between exegesis and biblical theology. Exegesis determines what the inspired text meant and what it means now. For this purpose, the exegete must believe that the Almighty God stands behind his word. There is no precise understanding of the Bible without faith in God. But this faith must not be divorced from human reason that can establish the meaning of the text through textual, historical, and literary evaluation. Harrington describes the relation between biblical theology and exegesis, "[e]xegesis is incomplete when it stops short of biblical theology, and biblical theology demands that exegetical scholarship should be ever conscious of the theological dimension of its task."[4]

For our purpose, we will approach the Bible from the perspective of faith that can understand the biblical records inspired by God. In this way we can perceive the inspired thoughts that relate to the overall plan of God with humankind, namely, salvation offered to all people. Accepting the revelation of God by faith in Jesus Christ will open up new possibilities of how to make God relevant today, especially to those who seemingly pay no attention to God. We will aim at exegesis of biblical words that relate to sports activities. We will proceed cautiously so that we satisfy the demands of a balanced approach of exegesis and biblical theology. The very beginning is in the Old Testament word study.

THE OLD TESTAMENT WORD STUDY

To fight, to do battle (*lacham*)

The Old Testament records many instances of fighting of nations and even individuals among themselves. The Hebrew word *lacham* appears throughout the Old Testament. Here are some representative passages. Exodus 14:14, "The Lord will fight for you; you need only to be still." Since the Israelites could not defeat the Egyptians on their own, they received a promise through Moses that the Lord would fight for them. Just try to imagine the Almighty God fighting against the whole Egyptian army and defeating the

Egyptians by drowning them in the Red Sea. Later Joshua describes his fight in Joshua 10:29, "Then Joshua and all Israel with him moved on from Makkedah to Libnah and attacked it." But the fighting was not over even during the period of Judges. We read in Judges 1:1-3, "After the death of Joshua, the Israelites asked the Lord, 'Who will be the first to go up and fight for us against the Canaanites?' The Lord answered, 'Judah is to go; I have given the land into their hands.' Then the men of Judah said to the Simeonites their brothers, 'Come up with us into the territory allotted to us, to fight against the Canaanites. We in turn will go with you into yours.' So the Simeonites went with them."

Another example is recorded in I Sam.17:10-11, "Then the Philistine said, 'This day I defy the ranks of Israel! Give me a man and let us fight each other.' On hearing the Philistine's words, Saul and all the Israelites were dismayed and terrified." But there was a man who had faith in God to help him fight the Philistine. His name was David and these were his words, "The Lord who delivered me from the paw of the lion and from the paw of the bear will deliver me from the hand of this Philistine (v.37).....This day the Lord will hand you over to me, and I'll strike you down and cut off your head. Today I will give the carcasses of the Philistine army to the birds of the air and the beasts of the earth, and the whole world will know that there is a God in Israel. All those gathered here will know that it is not by sword or spear that the Lord saves; for the battle is the Lord's, and he will give all of you into our hands" (vv. 46-47). The Lord did exactly what David believed. Goliath lost the battle and his life. And in Jeremiah 21:5 we have a record of God turning against his disobedient people and fighting against them, "I myself will fight against you with an outstretched hand and a mighty arm in anger and fury and great wrath." No wonder that Christians want God to be on their side and make them winners in sports. God can do anything for those who count on Him. If God does not help, they rationalize, it was not his will.

Christian athletes give credit to God for protecting them and giving them victory. They speak about it unashamedly, making God part of their fighting against their opponents. Coaches claim that, for instance, a football game is war and the players must fight to win. Chaplains ask God, with some caution, for help to win a game.

The concept of fighting is closely connected with sports. In fact, English generals made sure that during peace times soldiers would engage in sports to keep up their warlike mentality. It should be no strange activity for Christians to fight on the athletic fields and desire God's presence and his help. The Israelites counted on God. Christians should consider sports to be one of God's methods to win others for God's Kingdom. God does not shy away from helping us in fighting for the souls of people who have not heard the Good News about Jesus Christ.

To wrestle, to kick dust, to clasp around (abaq)

Wrestling is one of the major Olympic sports. Genesis 32: 24-32, Hosea 12:4, is a great story of God wrestling with Jacob. This passage portrayed Jacob leaving Laban and going to his relatives. He was going through the territory of his brother Esau who was waiting for him with a welcoming party of four hundred men. Jacob presupposed that this would be an occasion for Esau to have his revenge on him since Jacob tricked Isaac to bless him instead of Esau. Jacob was afraid for his family and for his own life. So he did the best thing under these circumstances – he prayed and sent gifts to Esau ahead of himself. Then he stayed behind alone, fearful, and distressed. What followed was a wrestling match with God. At first we read about a man who wrestled with Jacob till daybreak (v. 24), but later in the same chapter we learn that it was God whom Jacob saw face to face (v. 30).

In the darkest moment of his life, Jacob entered an extraordinary contest. He met God and wrestled with him in order to receive protection and blessing. Even after being hurt, he struggled so valiantly that God decided to change Jacob's name and his destiny. God told him, "Your name will no longer be Jacob, but Israel, because you have struggled with God and with men and have overcome" (v. 28). In this way, the promise of God to Abraham found its continuation. Truly, all nations on earth will be blessed through the future generations of Abraham. But for a moment there was some doubt about the outcome of the encounter between Jacob and Esau. Yet, God was fully in control. Because Jacob wrestled well with God and with men, the journey to Canaan was safe and the relationship with Esau was restored.

The exegesis of this text can provide vital lessons for us. First, when we wrestle with God during uncertain or dangerous times, we discover our limitations. Jacob's hip was wrenched, but his fighting spirit was undaunted. Notice the two sides of the battle. Jacob's body was hurt. He could have determined that because of his physical pain the struggle was over. But he behaved like a true athlete who disregards pain so that he would not lose a chance to win. Throughout history of sports some athletes finished races, matches, and games with pulled muscles and even broken bones. In these cases their spiritual and mental determination provided additional strength to continue. Both aspects of wrestling in the spiritual realm are important. We struggle with God and things might get worse. We desire the right things as we witness to people around us, but they are not paying much attention to us. Should we fold our efforts? No! We must keep on struggling and persevering in obeying the commands of our Lord. And God will notice. He will arrange our circumstances, especially when we admit our limitations in the area of seeing people accepting our Savior. We are limited in our struggle, but God, through His Spirit, can and will help. Why? God desires the salvation of all people and He entrusted to us the working out of his plan. Yes, we are limited in many ways, but we are not left without guidance and provisions.

Second, wrestling with God deepens our desire for God's blessings. We cannot overcome God. Jacob, the patriarch, did not. But while he was involved in this intense struggle, he realized that the only thing he could get out of it was to keep on wrestling well and be blessed by God. Jacob expressed it so well; "I will not let you go unless you bless me" (v. 26). The desire for God's blessing had a purifying effect. Jacob, the deceiver, became Israel, the one who struggled with God. Trickery was no longer his characteristic. He concentrated on the struggle and the need to be blessed by God. It is interesting to notice that God announced to Jacob that he was struggling not only with God, but with men as well. Jacob was a fighter in his relationship with Esau and later with Laban. This note provides room for an assertion that wrestling can be applied also to struggles among men. As we wrestle with God, He will equip us to wrestle with men and overcome them. The idea of overcoming can be applied to spiritual and physical realms where God-given victories are possible and where we can enjoy the blessings of God. Wrestling with God will prepare us for our struggles with men who need to hear about Christ. As Christians, we have to fight the good fight of faith. Jacob is an excellent example of how to prevail.

THE NEW TESTAMENT WORD STUDY

To compete in a contest in the arena (*athleo*)

Competition was on Paul's mind many times as he wrote letters to Christians. He did not separate living the Christian life from striving and making maximum effort. For Paul, following Christ meant placing oneself into the arena of the world and come out victoriously. He was sufficiently informed about the contests in the coliseums of the Roman world to make precise comparisons. These are his words to Timothy, his son in faith, "Endure hardship with us like a good soldier of Christ Jesus. No one serving as a soldier gets involved in civilian affairs – he wants to please his commanding officer. Similarly, if anyone competes as an athlete, he does not receive the victor's crown unless he competes according to the rules" (II Tim. 2:3-5). Paul's analogy of an athlete competing according to the rules and having the victor's crown placed on his head, is a clear picture of a Christian who lives the victorious life for Christ. There is just a small step from the spiritual to the secular. It makes sense to recommend Christians to step into stadiums, ball-parks, fields, and parks to engage our sports crazy culture to compete with those who do not accept our rules and regulations, but who might give in to our love, joy, peace, patience, kindness, goodness, faithfulness, gentleness, and self-control (Gal. 5:22-23). There are many possibilities in these contacts that are available to us if we are willing to compete for points and for souls at the same time.

To fight, struggle, strive (*agonizomai)*

Christians should be well acquainted with this word. Jesus used it in Luke 13:24, "Make every effort to enter through the narrow door, because many, I tell you, will try to enter and will not be able to." We are to struggle and strive daily to reach our goal of living lives that would be pleasing unto our Lord. We are not taking a sightseeing trip on earth for our own enjoyment. We have a higher calling. We must make sure that all people around us see something of Christ in us and that they also hear from us the Good News of salvation through faith in Christ. If they do not hear the gospel, they might try to enter the narrow gate according to their preconceived ideas only to be rejected because Christ will not know them as his followers.

Paul uses the word *struggle* concerning his own ministry, "We proclaim him, admonishing and teaching everyone with all wisdom, so that we may present everyone perfect in Christ. To this end I labor, struggling with all his energy, which so powerfully works in me" (Col. 1:28-29). Struggling is a vital part of the Christian life. Paul demonstrated this fighting spirit in his missionary service. His source of energy was God himself. That was the reason for the tremendous success and continuation of Paul's ministry till the very end.

He could honestly state, "I have fought the good fight, I have finished the race, I have kept the faith. Now there is in store for me the crown of righteousness, which the Lord, the righteous Judge, will award to me on that day – and not only to me, but also to all who have longed for his appearing" (II Tim. 4:7-8). Paul is alluding to a sport contest where the victor is awarded the victor's crown. He sees himself before God and rejoicing in being awarded the incorruptible crown.

But Paul demanded the same fight from other Christians as well. It was not reserved just for the few selected superstars of the Christian world. He made sure that Timothy would not miss out on the exciting part of living for Christ. So he challenged him, "Fight the good fight of faith. Take hold of the eternal life to which you were called when you made your good confession in the presence of many witnesses" (I Tim. 6:12). Here is a command. Fight to the point of intense physical and mental pain! Paul used the word *agona* because it was demonstrated in the fighting of athletes who desired to win.

What can we learn from the sports arena in order to understand our fight better? First, the athletes who want to win must take seriously their preparation for the fight. They participate in training camps that are more demanding physically and mentally than the expected games. Their bodies hurt because of the elevated demand on their muscles. They get hurt because they engage in dangerous moves. They collide with other bodies and have to get up and continue in their training. There is little room for rest and comfort. Some will not be able to take all that punishment and will go home losing their chance to compete. But those who will go through the agony, they will make the team and will compete.

It took forty years for Moses to go through the training camp in the desert, but then God called him to be on his team to lead the Israelites out of Egypt. It took fifty days of prayer, waiting, and fellowship before the early disciples received power when the Holy Spirit came on them. Timothy had to flee from sin and pursue righteousness in order to fight the good fight. Unless Christians take seriously the need for preparation, the power to win our world for Christ will be missing.

Second, there is no value in preparation to fight without engaging in the good fight. There are no happy athletes sitting on the sidelines. They want to compete. They want to prove themselves as winners. When football players get hurt, they want to know immediately how long it will take to get back on the field. They usually surprise their doctors by healing fast and well. They cannot stand being spectators. So many Christians behave contrary to athletes. They claim to be followers of Christ, but they resort to just watching others to do the fighting. No wonder we are not seeing enough victories. Spectator Christianity is not something Christ called us to. We are to engage this world and fight with God's help. We should be always asking, "Lord, which good fight am I to fight?" According to Paul, there are many struggles for Christians to accept, "For our struggle is not against flesh and blood, but against the rulers, against authorities, against powers of this dark world and against the spiritual forces of evil in heavenly realms. Therefore put on the full armor of God, so that when the day of evil comes, you may be able to stand your ground, and after you have done everything, to stand" (Eph. 6:12-13). We have ignored for too long the sports world, thinking that it was not appropriate for Christians. While we stayed away from sports, they became the predominant factor in our culture. We lost our fight by not engaging in it. We denied ourselves a good chance to make a difference among sports minded people. We let the powers of this dark world have freedom to form the development of sports culture.

There is a better way to approach this cultural phenomenon. We should give up our negative suppositions about sports and enter the arena with the positive mindset of winning this battle by joining the millions of people who are intoxicated by sports. Engaging in sports will give us an opportunity to introduce Christianity to the secularized and often violent world of sports. This should be nothing new for Christians. The first century world was a hostile place towards Christians but they did not shrink back. On the contrary, they proclaimed Christ in all places even though they ended in prisons, were flogged, thrown in front of wild animals, and were crucified for their faith. Yet, they won the battle, and Christ changed the world through them. Can we continue our separation from the world by limiting our witness to our sanctuaries in light of the early sacrifices of those brave fighters for faith? The answer is obvious and so the resolution on our part should be an effective search for the best involvement in the struggle that Paul mapped out for us.

Third, we must never forget that when we fight, we can expect a reward. The ongoing fight of Christians is in taking hold of the eternal life to which they are called. The athlete fights to win and expects to be the best in order to receive the gold medal. This is what keeps him on the right track and what pushes him beyond his limits. No sacrifice is too big. He expects his single-mindedness to be rewarded. Christians lose sight of their reward quite often. They serve God as if they are under pressure to do it. They sometime give up because of the lack of motivation, or a burnout. But such cases can be avoided if we understand the spiritual warfare. Our motivation should be even greater than that of athletes because our gold medal is the incorruptible crown. Paul writes about it in I Cor. 9:24-27, "Do you not know that in a race all the runners run, but only one gets the prize? Run in such a way as to get the prize. Everyone who competes in the games goes into strict training. They do it to get a crown that will not last; but we do it to get a crown that will last forever. Therefore I do not run like a man running aimlessly; I do not fight like a man beating the air. No I beat my body and make it my slave so that after I have preached to others, I myself will not be disqualified for the prize."

Paul must have been an athlete or at least he was an excited spectator of sports. His terminology betrays his enormous interest in sports like running and fighting - possibly boxing. These four verses in I Corinthians are very close to ideas on sports evangelism. Paul makes a correlation between athletes and Christians that should revolutionize our thinking on discipleship and witnessing. Running in the Christian race is a must in Paul's mind. The only question left is whether everyone gets the prize. Paul's explanation makes it clear that those who go into strict training and then run will receive the crown. Paul makes sure that his readers get the message about the difference in the reward of athletes and Christians. Athletes get gold medals, place them on a shelf at home and enjoy looking at them for many years.

Their memories are wonderful, but fleeting, especially if they are not capable of winning more medals. On the other hand, Christians do not have a visible crown displayed at home and therefore cannot boast about their victories. But the big difference is that their crown is on display in heaven and will be given to them by their Savior. No worldly superstar will be able to take his or her medal to heaven. Those medals are temporal and corruptible. Do we really comprehend what Paul is writing about in I Corinthians? Rethinking this concept should motivate many Christians to get involved in the good fight of faith in hope that they will receive the greatest possible reward.

Paul connects the good fight with taking hold of the eternal life in I Tim. 6:12. But knowing other writings of the apostle Paul will shed more light on the overall fight. In Phil. 3:10 he writes, "I want to know Christ and the power of his resurrection and the fellowship of sharing in his sufferings, becoming like him in his death." Jesus told Paul that he expected him to be a witness to the Gentiles and to suffer for His name. Paul's theology was sufficiently sound already in Damascus that he accepted the task and the fight before him. He had no regrets as he described it in sports-like terms in Phil. 3:14, "I press on toward the goal to win the prize for which God has called me heavenward in Christ Jesus."

What an example we have in Paul! He went through the stage of preparation in the company of Ananias and Barnabas. He engaged in the good fight of faith all his life as he witnessed about Christ and planted churches throughout his known world. His hope motivated him to persevere in order to win the prize. I can imagine that Paul used his knowledge of sports to his advantage as he boldly proclaimed Christ. It is high time to recover sports evangelism in our world.

To run *(trecho)*

The original usage of the word *trecho* was for the foot races in a stadium. Running races are probably the most exciting events at the Summer Olympic Games. Who would not enjoy watching the fastest man on earth to break the world or the Olympic record? And who would not get up to cheer for runners fighting for each centimeter in the final moment of the 1,500 meter race? The marathon race ends in the stadium for all to watch during the closing ceremony after covering a grueling distance of 42.195 kilometers. But *trecho* had also a figurative meaning of one who exerted himself to the limits of his powers in order to run forward to cross the finish line. Paul used it in this sense in Gal. 2:1-2, "Fourteen years later I went up again to Jerusalem, this time with Barnabas. I took Titus along also. I went in response to a revelation and set before them the gospel that I preach among the Gentiles. But I did this privately to those who seemed to be leaders, for fear that I was running or had run my race in vain." The same word occurs in Phil. 2:16, "As you hold out the word of life – in order that I may boast on the day of Christ that I did not run or labor for nothing."

The stadium, the running path, the countryside, or wherever people engage in running are ideal places to meet people who need to hear about Christ. Being in shape presupposes an effective encounter because people who get easily out of breath cannot talk. But then one can always ask for a break and resume the same activity after a time of friendly conversation.

To train, to exercise self-control like athletes (*egkrateuomai)*

Here is another sports term used in the Bible. Literally, it means to accept the rigorous demands of athletic training. And it is Paul again who includes it in his writings like I Cor. 9:25, "Everyone who competes in the games goes into strict training." The comparison is clearly seen as Paul mentions athletes who willingly give up any thought of comfort for the sake of intense training that would assure victory. Our culture produces millions of people who will train to the point of destroying their bodies so that they would look like Mr. or Mrs. Universe. Aerobics exercises flourish everywhere. Gyms are full in spite of monthly fees. Men and women go into strict training to be fit and to look like Olympians. Christians might not have as high goals as these muscle building athletes, but we need exercise as well. Signing up in a local gym is an easy assignment especially in January when all kinds of offers are in our mailboxes. Establishing a regular exercise program might be more difficult, but think about it this way. You will be able to see the same people over and over again in the same gym. This is a great opportunity to meet people of your community and point them to Jesus. And the byproduct of your exercise and sports evangelism could be a better figure as well.

To walk, go about *(peripateo)*

The Olympic athletes have to walk 50 kilometers to complete their race. Walking is a sport enjoyed by many as they venture out from their homes to get exercise. Jesus walked for miles while doing his ministry. "As Jesus was walking beside the Sea of Galilee, he saw two brothers,

Simon called Peter and his brother Andrew. They were casting a net into the lake, for they were fishermen. 'Come follow, me,' Jesus said, 'and I will make you fishers of men.' At once they left their nets and followed him" (Matt. 4:18-20). The leader of Christ's apostles signed up as Jesus walked by the lake. Continuing his walk, Jesus called two more brothers, James son of Zebedee and John. These two immediately left their father and their nets and followed their Lord. There are many opportunities for ministry as we pay attention to people who are next to us. Asking someone to go on a walk with you, presents a unique possibility for sharing the gospel. You might not be as efficient as Christ by calling great leaders to join the army of God, but the example is vivid before us. The only thing we need to do is to emulate Christ and fight the good fight of faith.

Reading the Bible from the perspective of sports evangelism supplied various passages relating to the subject. Even though the evidence is not quite direct, the usage of athletic terminology is unmistakable. Our approach was not only descriptive because that would not have served our purpose. Rather, we chose the path of biblical theology suggested by Childs, "Again, to speak of the canon as a context implies that these Scriptures must be interpreted in relation to their function within the community of faith that treasured them.

The Scriptures of the church are not archives of the past but a channel of life for the continuing church, through which God instructs and admonishes his people."[5] We live in a time when the interpretation of the Bible must reflect new cultural trends. Sports culture forms one of those trends. Our word study hopefully points us to engaging the sports culture while we can.

This task is not as simple as it sounds. Many writers are interested in the relationship of sports and Christianity. One of them is Robert Hicks who writes, "I will contend that sports and religion – I will mostly be thinking of Christianity – are in many ways incompatible. I would even argue that the ways in which modern sports have become entangled with religious practices constitute a (Christian) heresy, though this book will not focus on an argument for this judgment."[6] Yet, he goes on to argue his case by quoting Jack Saarela with whom he agrees, "I have problems with ministries that parade up winners on the stage – athletes, entertainers. The implication is if you accept Christ, you can be a winner, too. It's not any more honest than Madison Avenue saying if you want to be a winning person, drink certain beer. To me, Christianity is about a man who died on the cross. He was a loser. He appealed to the losers in society."[7] To call Jesus a loser reveals an incredible ignorance of the real story of

Jesus Christ. Jesus died on the cross, but he also rose from the dead thus achieving the greatest victory this world ever experienced.

Without Jesus Christ we would be left with the psalmist's conclusion in Psalm 89:47-48, "Remember how fleeting is my life. For what futility you have created all men! What man can live and not see death, or save himself from the power of the grave?" The psalmist was right – no man can defeat the power of the grave, but the God-man Jesus Christ. He is the resurrected and victorious Christ. His followers have confidence that even though they might not win every match or every game, they are winners from the perspective of eternal life with Christ. Paul declares this truth in Romans 8:34-37, "Who is he that condemns? Christ Jesus, who died – more than that, who was raised to life – is at the right hand of God and is also interceding for us. Who shall separate us from the love of Christ? Shall trouble or hardship or persecution or famine or nakedness or danger or sword? As it is written: 'For your sake we face death all day long; we are considered as sheep to be slaughtered.' No, in all these things we are more than conquerors through him who loved us."

There are some difficulties occurring as Christianity and sports mingle together. Christians have to be vigilant as they enter the arena of sports to represent the Lord Jesus Christ and to demonstrate his love for all people. In spite of criticisms, correct and incorrect, nobody can prevent Christians from having a positive outlook on life and competition as they participate in sports. Christians interacted with athletes in the first century and we must do it in the 21st century as well. The Christian presence and proclamation among sports minded people can prove to be the corrective influence that would help athletes to stay away from sinful practices. We are to give them the opportunity to believe in Christ who can help them to live holy and victorious lives.

CHAPTER THREE

A THEOLOGY OF SPORTS EVANGELISM

Moving from the biblical foundations for evangelism to a theology of sports evangelism requires a change in methodology. We will no longer focus on particular texts that contain athletic terminology. We will consider the larger picture of systematic theology where we will try to see the Bible as a whole while relating different concepts into a harmonious system. This will include a closer look into our present, changing culture with one eye on God's plan of salvation among us and with the other eye on the challenge of sports as an idol competing with the eternal God for the affection of human beings. Autrey warned, "Man is not the same as he was fifty years ago. It is essential for evangelism to be aware of this and to meet these changes with adequate language, modified methodology, and the unchanging gospel of Christ."[1] Autrey wrote these words in 1966 in his book *The Theology of Evangelism* and did not mention anything about sports evangelism, but he uncovered the threefold need for doing evangelism well.

First, the postmodern man has a real difficulty understanding the Christian Latin. He became a victim of the process of secularization that succeeded in taking biblical and metaphysical concepts out of his mind and language. The call for adequate language was a call for language that the postmodern man could understand. Cherished Christian terms like repentance, justification, sanctification, redemption, and others lost their precise meanings for the man outside the church. Even though we agree that the message of the Gospel must not be changed, we had better proclaim it in language that makes sense in the 21st century.

Second, our methodology must reflect a contemporary theology that relates to all people since we are sent unto all nations. There is a lurking danger here for theologians and practitioners of evangelism. They must not allow the pressures of society to warp their theology in order to employ a new methodology. For instance, in the case of sports evangelism, we might be so preoccupied with our intense desire to use sports to open up doors into the lives of famous athletes, that we lower our standards of Christian thinking and living and join them in sinful practices. There is a fine line between relating to secular people as true ambassadors of Christ and yet not turning them off. Sound theology will always provide solutions for our behavior. Drummond's words can help, "evangelism begins in theology, not in anthropology. Failure to come to grips with this foundational fact can easily result in some sort of 'evangelical humanism' that exalts human activity to the point of virtually leaving God's actions in evangelism out of the redemptive picture. This in turn precipitates evangelistic gimmicks, emotionalism, and even manipulation."[2] Yes, we can and should modify our methodology, but at the same time, we must not devise new patterns that would resemble more the practices of the sports world than those of the church. We will succeed in producing proper methodology as we uphold the unchanging message about Jesus Christ.

Third, the gospel of Jesus Christ was written 2,000 years ago, but does not need any corrections imposed by the secular man. Paul states in II Timothy 3:16-17, "All Scripture is God-breathed and is useful for teaching, rebuking, correcting, and training in righteousness, so that the man of God can be thoroughly equipped for every good work." Since God stands behind his word, there is no reason to change it. Accepting

God's word as it is, will guarantee being equipped for every good work, including sports evangelism. We have already considered different passages from the Old Testament and New Testament, but now we will try to understand the mind of God about the Christian evangelistic involvement in the world of sports culture.

THE REDEMPTIVE PLAN OF GOD THE FATHER

The source of our knowledge about God the Father and his part in the redemption plan comes ultimately from the Bible. There is no other fully reliable source. This is our belief and we will proceed on the basis of this supposition because it is not the purpose of this book to deal with the establishment of the authority of the Bible. Biblical exegesis uncovers the biblical material that we will process through the discipline of systematic theology into a coherent whole as to the need to engage in sports evangelism. The benefit of systematic theology rests in the fact that it can and must be reformulated for each generation as the need arises. Since the phenomenon of modern sports is a fairly new development, starting in the 19th century, it is surprising that not more theologians attempted to do theology from the perspective of sports. The reason for this omission might be because the world of sports is so secularized that keeping a distance proves to be more comfortable. Or that the criticism of sports by Christians has built up a high wall that would be hard to scale for a ghetto minded theologian. Or, finally, because of the lack of biblical materials that would directly address this subject.

Our purpose is to enter this area in order to discover the mind of God the Father as to the redemption of men so that we do not miss our part in it. From the biblical perspective it is clear that God has a plan that will not be disrupted or spoiled by any other power. Erickson defines God's plan, "as his eternal decision rendering certain all things which shall come to pass...The plan of God is like the architect's plans, drawn first in his mind and then on paper, according to his intention and design, and only afterward executed in actual structure. Or God may be thought of as being an athletic coach who has a carefully conceived game plan which his team seeks to carry out."[3] It is enjoyable to uncover athletic terminology in regard to God's activity in Erickson's book. His analogy pictures God as a coach who is capable of executing his plan along with his players. We will try to make the same point by stressing the responsibility of Christians to join God in realizing his redemptive plan through sports evangelism.

The plan of God with human beings was stated already in Genesis 3:15 as God revealed his plan of salvation to the serpent, "And I will put enmity between you and the woman, and between your offspring and hers; he shall crush your head, and you shall strike his heel." Even though the name of Christ is not mentioned here, we can trace the development of this promise to him. This study will confirm the mighty power of God to do what he promised. Eve bore three sons, but only Seth became the seed whose family was preserved through the flood and continued in Noah. Again, Noah had three sons, but only Shem was blessed by God to have descendants culminating in the birth of Abram through whom God decreed to bless all the nations of the earth. Next, God made sure that the lineage would continue, not through Ishmael, but through the belated birth of Isaac. The almighty God was in control through many generations in spite of dangerous situations and circumstances that threatened to thwart his plan. Finally, the promise was fulfilled in the miraculous birth of the second Adam, the Lord Jesus Christ. Keil and Delitzsch conclude, "Christ is the seed of the woman, who tramples Satan under his feet, not as an individual, but as the head both of the posterity of the woman which kept the promise and maintained the conflict with the old serpent before His advent, and also of all those who are gathered out of all nations, are united to Him by faith, and formed into one body of which He is the head (Rom. 16:20)."[4]

Is it possible that the original plan and promise would not be realized? The answer will depend upon the presuppositions of the one answering. For the Christian who believes in the authoritative word of God, the answer will reveal the efficaciousness of God. There is no doubt that God is powerful enough to do what he promised. Isaiah 46:10-11 declares God's words, "I make known the end from the beginning, from ancient times, what is still to come. I say: My purpose will stand, and I will do all that I please. From the east I summon a bird of prey; from a far-off land, a man to fulfill my purpose. What I have said, that I will bring about; what I have planned, that I will do." In the world where evil forces constantly oppose the plan of God, we might think that at least something could go wrong. Something could get out of control, as we see in our lives on many occasions. But this is not true about God. Isaiah announces the plan of God to crush Assyria that invaded Israel. Then he applies the same judgment to the world that would try to disrupt God's plan, "This is the plan determined for the whole world; this is the hand stretched out over all nations. For the Lord Almighty has purposed, and who can thwart him? His hand is stretched out, and who can turn it back" (Isaiah 14: 26-27)?

The conviction of the biblical writers was unmistakable. Nobody could oppose God including the evil powers of this world. The wise man Solomon put it this way in Proverbs 19:21, "Many are the plans in a man's heart, but it is the Lord's purpose that prevails." Does this mean that God is the sole Performer in our world? No! We might not always understand God's purposes and his ways of accomplishing them, but we are to be part of God's activity even though only secondarily. "For we are God's workmanship, created in Christ Jesus to do good works, which God prepared in advance for us to do" (Eph. 2:10). This thought brings a great encouragement to Christians who want to be obedient to God and who want to be involved in the redemptive plan of God. In our case the good works can be associated with the effort to befriend the secular people in sports environment in order to proclaim the Good News to them.

But we must not also forget to mention those works that are evil. Do they fit the overall plan of God? Finding and example that would shed some light on this possibility is not that difficult. Jesus faced betrayal, and crucifixion that proceeded seemingly according to the plan of evil men. And yet, these events were foreordained and included in the plan of God. Prophets revealed some of those evil deeds hundreds of years before they happened. Isaiah prophesied about Christ in chapter 53, "He was despised and rejected by men (v.3). But he was pierced for our transgressions, he was crushed for our iniquities; the punishment that brought us peace was upon him, and by his wounds we are healed" (v. 5). Zechariah predicted, "They will look on me, the one they have pierced, and they will mourn for him as one mourns for an only child, and grieve bitterly for him as one grieves for a firstborn son" (Zechariah 12: 10). Evil men and their deeds did not succeed to eliminate the plan of God written down in Genesis 3. On the contrary, men who opposed God will mourn and grieve, as their evil acts will be revealed during the coming of the Messiah in the future.

We are living in a time when God is still pursuing the original plan. There are no changes. The God who does not change is working out the specifics. We do not have to be afraid that while we desire to cooperate with God, he might change his mind. The examples from the prophets are sufficient to prove our point. But someone might object by reminding us of God's message delivered by Jonah of the impending judgment upon the people in Nineveh. "Forty more days and Nineveh will be overturned" (Jonah 4:4). This message was not a declaration of destruction; rather it was a warning to the Ninevites and it worked. The Ninevites believed God, repented of their wickedness and turned to God. The ultimate plan of God, namely the redemption of people, became a reality for all who lived in the city of Nineveh.

The apostle who was closest to Jesus Christ revealed a wonderful truth about God in his first letter, "Whoever does not love does not know God, because God is love. This is how God showed his love among us: He sent his one and only Son into the world that we might live through him" (I John 4:8). The propelling attribute behind the plan of God to save people is the fact that God is love. Without the love of God for men, the plan would have never been designed. The love of God endures forever (Psalm 100:5); therefore, the plan will be accomplished. Notice that the plan encompasses the whole world. It is not regional like many of our plans. Jesus proclaimed the all-encompassing scope of what God would accomplish, "For God so loved the world that he gave his one and only Son, that whoever believes in him shall not perish but have eternal life" (John 3:16).

Thinking about the enormous love of God should move us in the direction of sinful men. We are part of presenting salvation unto all people. There is no other option in place. We will either love the people around us by presenting the gospel to them, or we will ignore our responsibility to do it. Up to 95 percent of Christians are not involved in intentional evangelism; therefore, we must consider reasons for this disobedience.

Universalism

The position of universalism has been with the church since the writings of Origen (A.D. 185 – 254). As a respected church father, he managed to influence many believers with his writings. Drummond describes Origen's teaching this way, "Origen saw God's goodness as extending even to the divine desire that the devil be saved. Moreover, because God is just, all thinking beings have free will. Finally, God possesses such power that He can accomplish His purpose. Therefore, God in His goodness and justice purposes to save all thinking beings, and it will certainly be accomplished."[5] It took some time before the church would condemn the universalistic position of Origen during the Council of Constantinople in A.D. 543. But this decision of the church did not eliminate the teaching itself because it held certain sway upon those who wanted to keep thinking within the larger hope for the lost and for those who never heard of Christ. One of these theologians is Nels Ferre. He builds his theology on just one attribute of God that is love. Therefore his perception is narrow and misleading as he justifies his position by stating that love and punishment, heaven and hell are mutually exclusive. He explains, "Some have never really seen how completely contradictory are heaven and hell as eternal realities. Their eyes have never been opened to this truth. If eternal hell is real, love is eternally frustrated and heaven is a place of mourning and concern for the lost. Such joy and such grief cannot go together."[6]

The most damaging element of this teaching is in the fact that it proclaims in no uncertain terms that in the end God will accept all people into heaven because he loves them. If this is true, then the responsibility to evangelize is gone and the proponents of this position can falsely relax and do nothing about four billion unsaved people in our world. We have to admit that there are certain verses that can be used in the favor of a Universalist position. For instance, "we have put our hope in the living God, who is the Savior of all men, and especially of those who believed" (I Tim. 4:10); and "that at the name of Jesus every knee should bow, in heaven and on earth and under the earth, and every tongue confess that Jesus is Lord to the glory of the Father" (Phil. 2:10-11); and "For God has bound all men over to disobedience so that he may have mercy on them all" (Rom. 11:32).

These are not, however, the only verses that deal with this issue. As systematic theology demands, we must also look at verses that are on the opposite side of the spectrum. Then we can come up with an answer that will not violate the whole context of this problem. To find verses that speak against universalism is not that difficult. Here are some examples of words spoken by Jesus himself, "For God so loved the world that he gave his one and only Son, that whoever believes in him shall not perish but have eternal life" (John 3:16); "Then they will go away into eternal punishment, but the righteous to eternal life" (Matt. 25:46); "Do not be amazed at this, for a time is coming when those who are in their graves will hear his voice and come out – those who have done good will rise to live, and those who have done evil will rise to be condemned" (John 5:28-29). Next, are quotes from other books written by Paul and John, "What if God, choosing to show his wrath and make his power known, bore with great patience the objects of his wrath – prepared for destruction" (Romans 9:22)? "But the cowardly, the unbelieving, the vile, the murderers, the sexually immoral, those who practice magic arts, the idolaters and all liars – their place will be in the fiery lake of sulfur, This is the second death" (Rev. 21:8). We can list other verses just to prove there are many more like Matthew 8:12, Mark 3:29, Romans 2:5, 2 Thessalonians 1:9, but it will suffice to say that the verses used to propagate universalism are not as clear in their interpretation as those supporting the sound doctrine of salvation and judgment.

In the words of Erickson, the person believing in the universalist position, "ignores the fact that our inheriting eternal life involves two separate factors: an objective factor

(Christ' provision of salvation) and the subjective factor (our acceptance of that salvation)."[7] Whoever tries to do theology by choosing favorite verses to prove his point while ignoring others will run the danger of creating a misleading theology. The results can be far reaching causing malfunction in the life of the church. Universalism fits this scenario and has caused multitudes to give up on evangelism prematurely.

God's sovereignty and man's responsibility

There are those who believe that the plan of God to redeem people is firmly in God's hands and within his power; therefore there is no need to evangelize. We cannot make any difference. The elect will be saved and those who are not elected will perish. What God purposed, that will happen. Isn't this the right position of someone who trusts God? Well, it is only partially right. These Christians forget that God chose them to present the gospel even to the elect. Or how in the world can they be saved? Romans 10:14-15 addresses this issue, "How, then, can they call on the one they have not believed in? And how can they believe in the one of whom they have not heard? And how can they hear without someone preaching to them? And how can they preach unless they are sent? As it is written, 'How beautiful are the feet of those who bring good news!" Paul would not have accepted the position of simply trusting God with the salvation of the unsaved without bringing the gospel to them. He spent most of his Christian life going to all people he could reach with the good news. There is no way that a true follower of Christ can shake off the demand of God to present the gospel.

Even under the old covenant the people of God had the responsibility to warn the sinful and the wicked. Ezekiel received a command from God to warn those who would respond to his words and those who would not. Both groups had to hear from God. Here is the message that is applicable in our time as well, “Son of man, I have made you a watchman for the house of Israel; so hear the word I speak and give them warning from me. When I say to a wicked man, ‘You will surely die,’ and you do not warn him or speak out to dissuade him from his evil ways in order to save his life, that evil man will die for his sin, and I will make you accountable for his blood. But if you do warn the wicked man and he does not turn from his wickedness or from his evil ways, he will die for his sin; but you will have saved yourself” (Ezekiel 3:17-19). How much more is this true about our time since we know about the love of God revealed in Jesus Christ? If we truly appreciate the love of God revealed through his Son, we will not be silent. We must find ways how to approach the people around us. God will make us accountable. God will require the blood of those who did not hear from us. There is no room for any excuses here.

I remember a deacon in my church that proudly announced to me every time he saw me, "You know that I am a Calvinist." How could I forget? Not only that he reminded me of that belief so often, but also I could see the results of his conviction in the area of evangelism. He never joined me to visit a prospect for our church. He never brought a visitor to our church. And he did not see a need to witness to his son who was not a Christian. But I have to admit that he asked me to witness to him. He might have been a far out example of what hyper – Calvinism can do to a Christian, but these are the Christians who will not obey simple commands of Christ, "But you will receive power when the Holy Spirit comes on you; and you will be my witnesses in Jerusalem, and in all Judea and Samaria, and to the ends of the earth" (Acts 1:8); "Then Jesus came to them and said, 'All authority in heaven and on earth has been given to me. Therefore go and make disciples of all nations, baptizing them in the name of the Father and of the Son and of the Holy Spirit, and teaching them to obey everything I have commanded you. And surely I am with you always, to the very end of the age' "(Matt. 28:18-20). Again, there is no way around these words of our Savior Jesus Christ.

No theological conviction should prevent us from obediently doing evangelism. Leighton Ford gives an appropriate suggestion, "We must avoid the temptation either to an exclusive concern with human responsibility (which makes us panicky and alarmist), or to an exclusive concern with divine sovereignty (which can make us cynical about all evangelical endeavors)."[8] Either option can hinder evangelism even though the latter can even prevent desired evangelistic effort. When we organize events where sports evangelism can happen, we must heed Ford's warning not to think that everything depends on us and our talents in sports otherwise we could resort to success oriented evangelism where we fabricate results through emotional manipulation. There is only a small step from trusting the sovereign God to taking things into our own hands so that we can receive the glory for cleverly organized sports events.

Nominal Christianity

Every denomination is marked by membership of people who are not Christians. Our low standard for accepting new members into our churches has caused this problem. Nominal Christians are not true followers of Christ. They just accepted the name Christian, not really understanding what it means. Can we be surprised that these church members are not interested in evangelism? Certainly not! They have never really experienced the love of God through a personal relationship with Jesus. How can they then witness about him? They have no desire and no motivation to be witnesses. Ford quotes Samuel Shoemaker as he expressed his dissatisfaction with the state of church membership in America, "I am shocked to find out how many people in our churches have never anywhere made a decisive Christian commitment. They oozed into church membership on a conventional kind of basis, but no one has ever effectively dealt with them spiritually, or helped them make a Christian decision."[9] E. Stanley Jones describes nominal Christians from the theological perspective, "Our churches are filled with people who know about Christ, but do not know Him; are informed about Christ, but are not transformed by Him; know about the moral laws, but are powerless to fulfill them."[10] What is needed here is a conversion experience so that nominal Christians would become God's children who would be equipped by the Holy Spirit to evangelize people around them. If this situation persists, we must not be surprised that this obstacle is firmly in place.

From the biblical perspective, it should not be difficult to establish certain guidelines to prevent nominal Christianity. Being religious is not identical with being a Christian.

Nicodemus was a Pharisee and a member of the Jewish ruling council. He was impressed with the miraculous signs Jesus performed, so he showed up at night to secretly meet with him. Jesus did not acknowledge Nicodemus' status in the religious community in Jerusalem. He was not especially impressed with his polite words. Jesus was concerned above all with the spiritual status of Nicodemus. Therefore, he told him rather confrontationally, "I tell you the truth, no one can see the kingdom of God unless he is born again" (John 3:3). Verse seven repeats the same message, "You should not be surprised at my saying, 'You must be born again'."

I wonder how many local churches would welcome the influential, religious man into their membership without even asking for a testimony of being born again. As a matter of fact, many churches are satisfied simply with a letter of recommendation coming from the previous church, never trying to find out whether the man, or the woman, is saved. This is not a biblical practice and it does more harm than good. Paul cuts to the root of this issue in Galatians 6:15, "Neither circumcision nor uncircumcision means anything; what counts is a new creation." When we emphasize regenerate membership, we will have removed most of the obstacle caused by nominal Christians.

Specialized ministry

Many Christians think falsely that the task of evangelism is only for the clergy and for the church staff. This escapism is nourished by the idea that the full time workers should reach secular people. They are educated and trained, so why don't they do it. The lay people will not say it openly, but they think that because they give money to the church, ministers should be evangelizing on their own. The message is loud and clear, especially when we know that only 3 to 5 percent of church members are consistently involved in evangelistic visitation.

The Bible presents a different picture. Peter describes the church in his first letter 2:9, "But you are a chosen people, a royal priesthood, a holy nation, a people belonging to God, that you may declare the praises of him who called you out of darkness into his wonderful light." Christians are a royal priesthood. We are all priests who are to introduce secular people to Jesus as we declare the good news about our Savior. There is no division of ministry in this area. Jesus expects that because of his power in us through the indwelling Holy Spirit, all Christians, not just the few ordained ministers, will be his witnesses (Acts 1:8).

Christians in the first century lived up to the expectation of their Savior and changed their world. It took about three centuries before Christianity was accepted by the Roman Empire as a legitimate religion due to the determination of God's people to witness and to penetrate their culture. Jesus did not change his mind on the need for us to be his witnesses to the ends of the earth. Yet, we are failing miserably at this task. A modern day movement spread very fast after hearing the challenge of Karl Marx who said, "Philosophers have only interpreted the world differently; the point is to change it." Marxists and Communists changed two thirds of our world using violence, intimidation, persecution, and murder. The end of the 20th century saw the collapse of Communism in most parts of the world. Now is the time for Christians to regain the vision of changing our world for Christ again. But church professionals will not accomplish it alone. It will take all Christians to permeate every corner of all nations in the power of the Holy Spirit. Sports evangelism can facilitate inroads into places where we are not even present right now.

THE SEEKING OF GOD THE SON AFTER THE LOST

Incarnation

The redeeming plan of God was set in motion in the Garden of Eden. The future Victor over the Evil One would come to this earth to complete the work of salvation. Therefore, the incarnation of God became an absolute necessity. God had to be made flesh so that the ultimate sacrifice would happen and be acceptable to the righteous God, "And the Word became flesh and made his dwelling among us. We have seen his glory, the glory of the One and Only, who came from his Father, full of grace and truth" (John 1:14). Jesus, the Son of God, did not hesitate to come into our world to show the love of God to men who needed forgiveness of their sins. To take this lightly would be a gross misunderstanding of the mission of Christ. He left the glory of heaven, the beauty of fellowship with his Father and the Holy Spirit, and he entered this dirty ball flying through a tiny space in the universe to experience poverty of a stable, rejection of ignorant people, hostility from the rulers of his time, short lived fellowship with the twelve among whom there was a traitor, ingratitude of some of those whom he healed, misunderstandings of his teachings, and finally a horrible death on the cross. Could there have been another way to provide salvation for us? McRainey tells a parable that sheds some light on a possible answer.

> This is about a modern man, one of us. He was a Scrooge. He was kind, decent, mostly good man.

He was generous to his family, upright with his dealings with other men, but he did not believe in all that incarnation stuff which the churches proclaim at the Christmas time. It just didn't make sense, and he was too honest to pretend otherwise. He just could not swallow the Jesus story and God's coming to earth as a man. "I am truly sorry to distress you." He told his wife, "but I am not going with you to church this Christmas Eve." He said he'd feel like a hypocrite, so he would much rather stay home. He stayed. They went.

Shortly after the family drove away, snow began to fall. He went to the window to watch the flurries getting heavier and heavier and then went back to his fireside chair to read his newspaper. Minutes later he was startled by a thudding sound, then another, then another. At first he thought someone must be throwing snowballs against his living room window. When he went to the front door to investigate, he found a flock of birds huddled miserably in the snow. They had been caught in the storm and in a desperate search for shelter had tried to fly through his large landscape window. He had compassion for them and wanted to help them. He couldn't let the poor creatures lie there and freeze.

He remembered the barn where his children stabled their pony that would provide a warm shelter if he could direct the birds into it. He quickly put on his coat and galoshes and tramped through the deepening snow to the barn. He opened the doors wide and turned on a light. But the birds did not come in. He figured food would entice them in. He hurried back to the house to fetch bread crumbs to sprinkle on the snow, in order to make a trail to the yellow-lighted wide-open doorway of the stable.

But to his dismay the birds ignored the bread crumbs and continued to flop around helplessly in the snow. He tried catching them. He tried shooing them into the barn by walking around them waving his arms. Instead they scattered in every direction – except into the warm, lighted barn. Then he realized they were afraid of him. "To them," he reasoned, "I am a strange and terrifying creature. If only I could think of some way to let them know they can trust me, that I'm not trying to hurt them, but to help them." How? Any move he made tended to frighten them, confuse them. They just would not follow. They would not be led or shooed because they feared him.

He thought, *If I could mingle with them and speak their language and tell them not to be afraid and show them the way to the safe, warm barn. But I'd have to be one of them so they could see and hear and understand. If only I could be a bird myself.*

At that moment, the church bells began to ring. The sound reached his ears above the sounds of the wind. He stood there listening to the bells playing "Adeste Fidelis," pealing the glad tidings of Christmas. And he sank to his knees in the snow. At last, he understood God's heart towards mankind, and he fell on his knees in the snow. He had come to know the One who became one of us just to save us.[11]

It is not possible for a man to become a bird. But God became man. Those who do not believe in God, flatly deny incarnation. Those who have tasted the love of God do believe that God became flesh because with God all things are possible. Even though incarnation seems incredible, it was the only way in which salvation could have been offered to humans. God lived among us, spoke our language and revealed himself to us. Peters described the purpose of incarnation, "Christ Jesus came to deal effectively with sin, to become the atonement for sin, the liquidator of man's guilt, as well as the Conqueror and Annihilator of sin."[12] This thought leads us to the consideration of the necessity of Christ's death on the cross.

The Cross of Christ

The cross was central to the purpose of Christ, "For even the Son of man did not come to be served, but to serve, and to give his life as a ransom for many" (Mark 10:45). Christ explained further the necessity of the cross when he said, "Just as Moses lifted up the snake in the desert, so the Son of Man must be lifted up, that everyone who believes in him may have eternal life" (John 3:14-15). The way to eternal life opened up through the sacrificial death of Christ on the cross for all who believed in Christ.

The interpretation of the cross is vital to sound theology. Those who understand the cross, they understand who Jesus is. Therefore, the question of atonement is relevant: Why did Christ die? Paul writes, "God made him who had no sin to be sin for us, so that in him we might become the righteousness of God" (2 Cor. 5:21). The important word here is 'substitution'. Christ died in our place and consequently satisfied the demands of the holy and righteous God. Christ bore the penalty for our sins the Law of God demanded. Drummond states three reasons for Christ's death on the cross, "(1) because of the hostility of the Jewish religious leaders, (2) to effect the fulfillment of Scriptures, for example, Isaiah 53, Psalm 22, and (3) by his own choice, the Son of man personally determined to be also the "Suffering Servant." The dominant motivation in Jesus' ministry was Calvary."[13] The cross represents the greatest event in human history. It is not just another human happening. God himself died there instead of us. God himself proved his love for us. No wonder we changed the way we count years to start over again in order to make Christ the central figure of human history. P. T. Forsyth expressed it well, "Christ is to us just what his cross is. All that Christ was in heaven or on earth was put into what he did there."[14] We cannot fully understand the tremendous significance of the cross from merely human perspective. All of heaven paid attention. But God the Father did not intervene otherwise his redemptive plan would have been jeopardized.

The substitutionary death of Christ was absolutely necessary so that we could be redeemed. Without the cross we would be dying in our sins because of our total depravity. God would have to judge us because he is righteous, but because he is love as well, he provided the only perfect sacrifice for us, "But God demonstrates his love for us in this: While we were still sinners, Christ died for us. Since we have now been justified by his blood, how much more shall we be saved from God's wrath through him" (Romans 5:8-9). I like Paul's often repeated phrase 'how much more'. It expresses the richness of all that Christ did for us. We can rest in our relationship with Christ. His sacrificial death is sufficient for our salvation. Christ announced the completeness of his saving work from the cross, "It is finished" (John 19:30). We must be ever thankful for his ultimate sacrifice that shows the love of God in its fullness, "This is love: not that we loved God, but that he loved us and sent his Son as an atoning sacrifice for our sins" (I John 4:10). When men ask us what God is like, we can answer with certainty. Our God knows the pain and sorrows of men. Our God offers forgiveness of sins so that we are not condemned. And our God offers eternal life because he himself defeated death.

Resurrection

If Jesus simply died of old age and then rose from the dead on the third day, there would be no hope for us. Resurrection without the cross would not save us. But the cross without the resurrection would make Jesus a liar. Jesus predicted his resurrection, "From that time on Jesus began to explain to his disciples that he must go to Jerusalem and suffer many things at the hands of the elders, chief priests, and teachers of the law, and that he must be killed and on the third day be raised to life" (Matt. 16:21). This was public knowledge. Even the chief priests and the Pharisees knew about it, "we remember that while he was still alive that deceiver said, 'After three days I will rise again'" (Matt. 27:63).

The strongest evidence for the resurrection of Christ is the transformation of his disciples. They left their Master while he was hanging on the cross. Some were so afraid that they would not stay in Jerusalem. They wanted to forget those three great years with Christ and start over doing something else. These defeated disciples became bold preachers of the Good News of the resurrected Christ. If they did not see him alive, they would have never risked their lives for a lie. Yet, they proclaimed Christ wherever they went. Peter, who denied him prior to the crucifixion, declared clearly in his first sermon, "This man was handed over to you by God's set purpose and foreknowledge; and you, with the help of wicked men, put him to death by nailing him to the cross. But God raised him from the dead, freeing him from the agony of death, because it was impossible for death to keep its hold on him" (Acts 2:23-24). This is our message even in our times.

We must not give in to the age of postmodernism where seemingly there is no absolute truth. The words of Christ are truthful right now, "I am the resurrection and life. He who believes in me will live, even though he dies; and whoever lives and believes in me will never die. Do you believe this" (John 11:25-26)? The early Christians embraced this truth and made it the content of their message. Read the words of Paul, "For what I received I passed on to you as of first importance: that Christ died for our sins according to the Scriptures, that he was buried, that he was raised on the third day according to the Scriptures" (I Cor. 15:3-4). It is up to us to propagate the fact that Christ is alive in us. Why is it then that so many Christians never speak up for Christ? Whenever this is happening, Christ is displeased with his followers. We must be bold enough to witness. The reality of the resurrection should propel us to make the living Christ known.

Ascension

The ascension of Christ from this earth to heaven should help us in evangelism. Jesus predicted his ascension, "I came from the Father and entered the world; now I am leaving the world and going back to the Father" (John 16:28). On the slopes of Mount Olive, Christ fulfilled his prediction. A cloud hid him as he was taken up in front of the eyes of his followers. At that moment, two angels delivered an important message to them, “Men of Galilee, why do you stand here looking into the sky? This same Jesus, who has been taken from you into heaven, will come back in the same way you have seen him go into heaven” (Acts 1:11). There is no time for just looking into heaven. We are to be witnesses about Christ to the ends of the earth. We are to make sure that every person on the face of this earth will hear the gospel that is so precious to us. While obeying Christ’s command, we should act like those first disciples. Luke made sure to record their attitude for us, “Then they worshiped him and returned to Jerusalem with great joy. And they stayed continually at the temple praising God” (Luke 24:52-53). Joy and praise are the essential elements in the lives of those who know the living Christ. There is no room for sadness and disappointment. The Lord is not with us on this earth. But he finished the work of salvation and everything keeps on working according the plan of God. Right now Jesus is preparing a place for us in heaven, “Do not let your hearts be troubled. Trust in God; trust also in me. In my Father’s house there are many rooms; if it were not so, I would have told you. I am going there to prepare a place for you. And if I go and prepare a place for you, I will come back and take you to be with me that you also may be where I am” (John

14:1-3). Therefore, we should rejoice and accept our task to make Christ known. That is exactly what the apostles did. Pentecost came after ascension. We cannot improve on the attitudes of the first Christians, but we can emulate them.

Remember that we have the same Spirit living in us. Jesus taught this truth to his disciples, "But I tell you the truth: it is for your good that I am going away. Unless I go away, the Counselor will not come to you; but if I go, I will send him to you" (John 16:7). Sometimes I wish I would have been among those who had walked with Jesus through the streets of Jerusalem. But then I realize that I am in a better position now because wherever I go, Christ's Spirit is with me. He is with me always and the possibility is to do even greater things than Jesus did (John 14:12). Are we living up to this possible mission? My contention is that we are failing in this area for a very simple reason: we are neglecting the Holy Spirit in us.

THE POWER OF GOD THE HOLY SPIRIT TO SAVE THE LOST

Karl Barth was asked by his students about theological issues that, in his opinion, would be important in the future of the church. He challenged them to formulate the doctrine of the Holy Spirit. Why did he choose this doctrine?

The Holy Spirit is the neglected person of the Trinity. We believe in the Father, the Son, and the Holy Spirit, but we pay much more attention to God the Father and to Jesus Christ than to the Holy Spirit. Pentecostal Christians are not guilty of this negligence; however, their doctrine of the Holy Spirit elevates speaking in tongues to a level that is supposedly normative for all Christians. By doing so, they seem to demand speaking in tongues for all Christians in order to have the proof of being filled with the Holy Spirit. Such a doctrine is not found in the Bible and should be corrected in order to invite all Christians to experience the fullness of the Holy Spirit as it is available by the Holy Spirit himself and not through eager Christians who are willing to force the gift of speaking in tongues on others. They do this by overlooking the fact that in I Corinthians 12:11 we read, "All these are the work of one and the same Spirit, and he gives them to each one, just as he determines." Is it possible that because of some non-biblical emphases from Pentecostal believers, other Christians stay away from the command of Paul to be filled with the Spirit (Ephesians 5:18)? Are we afraid of that which should and could be our daily experience? I will try to explain that there is nothing to be afraid of; on the contrary, there is much to be gained by being obedient to the command of God.

I was raised in Czechoslovakia where under the Communistic government the Pentecostals were not allowed to exist as a denomination. So these believers would be visiting Baptist churches and infiltrating them with their Pentecostal theology. It usually did not take much time before they would gain some members for their house meetings where they emphasized and demonstrated speaking in tongues so that these newcomers would experience the second blessing of the Christian life. This kind of behavior caused mistrust in relation to these Pentecostal believers. Fear of excessive emotionalism caused Baptist preachers to be silent on just about everything that concerned the Holy Spirit. They just hoped that their silence would make this problem go away. That was not a good solution. On the contrary, it resulted in pervasive ignorance about the Holy Spirit among Baptists, and I was one of them.

Encountering another approach toward the Holy Spirit was equally damaging. It happened while I studied in the International Baptist Seminary in Ruschlikon, Switzerland. I was listening to a lecture by a German professor of the Old Testament. He was explaining some details about dates in the Old Testament and then he stated, "If we take this passage as it is written, then we can say that the Holy Spirit is not good with numbers." Even though I did not hear enough about the Holy Spirit from the pulpit, by this time I had read the Bible several times from the first page to the last page, and I knew immediately that talking about the Holy Spirit in this way was contrary to what the Bible said about the Holy Spirit. So I stood up and told that professor that I did not appreciate his description of the Holy Spirit as Someone who was not capable to produce right numbers. But I was the only one in that classroom who was bothered by that statement. Right there I had to deal with arrogance in regard to the Holy Spirit.

But that was not all. After three semesters in Switzerland, I moved to Tulsa, Oklahoma where I was awarded a full scholarship for playing tennis for Oral Roberts University. I did not know much about that university, but that was the only place where I was offered free education. Upon arrival, I knew that ORU was just the opposite of Ruschlikon. People were friendly, loving, and joyful. At first I did not know what was going on. Why were these people so nice to me? Was it because of the announcement in the chapel about a new Czech tennis player who just joined the team? Or was it because these people really loved Jesus and that love spilled over to others as well? Fairly soon I discovered that the people on the campus where talking a lot about the infilling of the Holy Spirit that empowered their lives.

I became curious because this was the first positive input I was receiving concerning the Holy Spirit. Instead of forming my opinion on the basis of what I heard at ORU and what I experienced there in the fellowship of students, I started my search in the Bible. This is what I learned.

The Holy Spirit is a Person.

We have no problem thinking about God the Father as a Person. He loved us enough to send his Son Jesus to live among us. We know that his love for us endures forever. Therefore, we come to him in prayer, address him as our Father and continue in this relationship. When we disobey him, we are aware of the possibility to confess our sins and to receive his forgiveness. Relating to God the Father seems quite natural because it resembles our relationship with our parents.

Our relationship with Christ is equally real. We appreciate his coming to this earth and remind ourselves of it each year at Christmas. We have the Gospels to read and to gain detailed information about his life and teachings. He died for our sins, but he also rose from the dead never to die again. His promise to be with us always, to the very end of the age, is true and we enjoy his presence with us.

But how is it with the Holy Spirit? He did not become flesh. He is likened to oil, fire, wind and a dove. No wonder that some Christians have a hard time relating to him. But when we study the Bible with the idea of getting to know the Holy Spirit, we find that he is called a Comforter (Parakletos) in John 14:16. He is the One who is called to our side. He offers his help through teaching, reminding, guiding, testifying, and glorifying Jesus (John 14-16). As a Person, he hears us and speaks with us, "But when he, the Spirit of truth, comes, he will guide you into all truth. He will not speak on his own; he will speak only what he hears, and he will tell you what is yet to come" (John 16:13). This information should encourage us to approach the Holy Spirit in the same way as we do the Father and the Son. In fact, the Bible uses interchangeably the names for the Spirit as the Spirit of God (Romans 8:9) and the Spirit of Christ (Acts 16:7). There is no competition within the Trinity. We should learn to relate to the Father and the Son and the Holy Spirit in the same way. There is, however, a need for distinction within the Trinity in regard to the functions of each Person of the Godhead. Paul writes in Galatians 4:6, "Because you are sons, God sent the Spirit of his Son into our hearts." God sent the Spirit of his Son as a response to the request of his Son to do so, "And I will ask the Father, and he will give you another Counselor to be with you forever" (John 14:16). The Holy Spirit is with us now and in this sense is vitally involved in our Christian lives. What a shame it is for any Christian to neglect this Comforter, especially in the light of the next point.

The Holy Spirit lives in every Christian.

The presence of the Holy Spirit is not reserved just for special children of God. Paul writes to Timothy, "Guard the good deposit that was entrusted to you – guard it with the help of the Holy Spirit that lives in you" (II Timothy 1:14). Peter challenged a large group of people who listened to his sermon, "Repent and be baptized, everyone of you, in the name of Jesus Christ for the forgiveness of your sins. And you will receive the gift of the Holy Spirit" (Acts 2:38).

Our neglect begins right here. We are not sure how to define this presence of the Holy Spirit in us. We ask questions: "Where does he live in me?" "How do I know he lives in me?" "How can I be sure this is true?" "Is it possible to prove this matter?" "If I do not feel the presence of the Holy Spirit, is he still living in me?" Doubts enter our minds when we do not have definite answers, and so the easiest thing to do is to forget about the Holy Spirit. Maybe this whole thing is just for those who are capable of mystical experiences, but we can do without them.

Even though we do not understand everything about the Holy Spirit, the Bible is clear on the fact that he is real. Paul goes as far as to claim, "And if anyone does not have the Spirit of Christ, he does not belong to Christ" (Romans 8:9). The presence of the Holy Spirit is the distinguishing mark of those who placed their trust in Jesus Christ. Your full theological understanding is not what qualifies you to receive the gift of the Holy Spirit. It is your faith in Christ. Once we believe in Christ, we are sealed with the Holy Spirit for the day of redemption, "And do not grieve the Holy Spirit of God, with whom you were sealed for the day of redemption" (Ephesians 4:30). We are no longer our own. We belong to God and He is making sure that we are living a life that is transformed by the Holy Spirit in us. A transformed life is the evidence of the presence of the Holy Spirit. I will describe this truth in my next point.

The Holy Spirit fills every Christian.

At first, we have to establish the fact that God planned the outpouring of the Holy Spirit already in the time of Joel, "And afterward I will pour out my Spirit on all people" (Joel 2:28). Peter quoted Joel in his sermon at Pentecost making sure that his audience would understand that the prophecy of Joel was now fulfilled. Christians were filled with the Holy Spirit through a mighty act of God. Later on Peter went to preach the same gospel to the Gentiles in the house of Cornelius and all those people believed in Jesus and were filled with the Holy Spirit just as the apostles at Pentecost (Acts 10:47). This was such an important event that Luke mentioned it three times in the Book of Acts – 10:47, 11:15, and 15:7-9. Did he forget from one chapter to another? No, but he used this repetition for emphasis. Something momentous happened here. The Gentiles believed and were filled with the Holy Spirit. The Spirit was not given just to the Jews, but also to the Gentiles. This was done so that all people would have the opportunity to be blessed by the infilling presence of the Holy Spirit.

There is an important lesson for us to learn here. Pentecostals teach the so called 'second blessing' which means that a believer receives the Holy Spirit at the time of his conversion, but he has to wait for the infilling at a later time. Usually there are conditions attached to this infilling, as if a believer had to earn it through his own efforts of greater faith, obedience, thorough cleansing of all known sin, consistent prayer, and a deep desire. The immediate question arises, "How can we be sure that we have satisfied these conditions?"

If we have to work our way toward the second blessing, then we can force God to give it to us based on our efforts. If that does not happen, even after our honest effort, we are left perplexed and unfulfilled. Do you think that God would welcome us into his family and then assign us an undetermined period of observation to decide if we really deserve to be filled with his Spirit? Do you really think that God the Father would say that our faith in his Son is not quite enough and that he will wait with the blessing of his full presence in us? This way of thinking does not quite compare with the idea of God that is revealed in the Bible. Because of our commitment to follow Jesus, we are born again. We experience the most beautiful beginning we can imagine. Peter is describing it in the most vivid terms in Acts 15:8-9, "God, who knows the heart, showed that he accepted them by giving the Holy Spirit to them, just as he did to us. He made no distinction between us and them, for he purified their hearts by faith."

Here we have Peter's explanation of what happens when people are filled with the Holy Spirit. Notice that God knows what is in the heart, yet he is willing to accept us since he purifies our hearts because of our faith in Christ. When the heart is pure, the stage is set for the giving of the Holy Spirit. There are no words about a partial giving of the Holy Spirit. There are no other conditions. God himself completely cleanses the heart. And what is equally important is the fact that the cleansing and the giving happen at the same time.

Peter used two simultaneous aorist participles, *dous* and *katharisas,* for the purpose of describing an instantaneous action. Based on this understanding of the Greek text, God is the One who purified their hearts and gave them his Spirit in the same way as he did it at Pentecost. Yes, these Gentiles were filled the same way as the apostles. No conditions were met. Frederick Bruner explains the infilling with the Holy Spirit in the house of Cornelius in this way, "Thus we may say to the Pentecostal conditions from this important text: the 'heart-cleansing' which is so painfully pursued God achieves; the faith which is so assiduously cultivated God grants; the Holy Spirit who is so scrupulously sought God gives – and the means is simply the divine gospel which is the power of God unto salvation (cf. Rom. 1:16)."[15]

Since we are Gentiles, this event applies to us. We can trust God that our faith in Christ brought about the same, instantaneous infilling with the Holy Spirit. But there can be an objection raised especially from Pentecostals in regard to this conclusion. They would say that as long as such an event is not accompanied with the speaking in tongues, there was no infilling. Is this a legitimate objection? No! There are eight instances of the infilling with the Holy Spirit described in the Book of Acts, but speaking in tongues is mentioned only three times (2:4, 10:45-46, 19:6). The other passages speak twice about boldness (4:31, 13:9), once about healing (9:17-18), once about preaching (4:8), and once about joy (13:52). There is no set pattern that we could follow or demand. We should remember the words of the apostle Paul when he writes, "Where the Spirit of the Lord is, there is liberty" (II Corinthians 3:17). We do the best when we submit to the Holy Spirit and let Him work in us according to his power and wisdom. He is capable of doing mighty things through us if we are continually filled with him.

The Holy Spirit demands that we be continuously filled with him.

Paul, inspired by the Holy Spirit, writes, "Be filled with the holy Spirit" (Ephesians 5:18). The word *plerousthe* can be translated "be habitually filled". This means that in the life of all Christians should be subsequent fillings with the Holy Spirit. This was true of Peter who was filled with the Holy Spirit at Pentecost (2:4), then when he spoke before the Sanhedrin (4:8), and, as far as we know, after his release from prison when he met with the rest of the disciples (4:31). There are three references to Paul concerning the infilling with the Holy Spirit: at conversion (9:17), at Paphos (13:9), and at Iconium (13:52). If these mighty apostles were filled with the Holy Spirit repeatedly, we should experience similar infillings as well.

Again, we have no definite procedure described in the Bible concerning these subsequent fillings with the Holy Spirit, but we have the command, "be filled with the Spirit". These words do not relate to the initial infilling with the Holy Spirit because Paul was writing to Christians. The need for subsequent infillings comes from the fact that we are capable of resisting the Holy Spirit. That is why Paul commands us, "And do not grieve the Holy Spirit of God, with whom you were sealed for the day of redemption. Get rid of all bitterness, rage and anger, brawling and slander, along with any form of malice" (Ephesians 4:30-31). Any action that is contrary to the guidance of the Holy Spirit, is detrimental to the infilling of the Holy Spirit.

But Paul gives us another command, "Do not put out the Spirit's fire" (I Thessalonians 5:19). We can harm our fellowship with the Holy Spirit and we can also quench him. Remember that the Holy Spirit is symbolized by fire. Our idleness, immorality, and routine worship will put out the fire of the Holy Spirit. We will become weak, discouraged, timid, and useless. Do you want that? I hope that you want to do something about it.

We can come to God confessing our sins. He will hear us and purify our hearts. We will experience the blessedness of those whose hearts are pure. God will repeat the miracle of infilling us with his Spirit again. And when that happens, we will impact the people around us. Our nation will not be able to ignore us.

When we are filled with the Holy Spirit, we will have students coming to professors asking them to take them to mission fields, rather than professors begging students to accept the burden of winning people to Christ. And ultimately, just like the apostles, we will be bold in proclaiming Christ and living for Him. This can be accomplished because of the infilling presence of the Holy Spirit in us that will bring glory to Christ.

In 1727 the Moravian believers experienced their own Pentecost. Out of this work of God among them came 220 missionaries that ministered throughout the world. The modern mission movement began. They also started a 24 hours a day prayer chain that lasted 100 years. God is ready to fill us again. Let us yield to the Spirit of God who wants to fill us and use us so that Christ would be glorified in our lives.

The Holy Spirit convicts non-Christians

People cannot save themselves. It is the work of the Holy Spirit, "When he comes, he will convict the world of guilt in regard to sin and righteousness and judgment: in regard to sin, because men do not believe in me; in regard to righteousness, because I am going to the Father, where you can see me no longer; and in regard to judgment, because the prince of the world now stands condemned" (John 16:8-10). Christians in sports arenas have to learn how to depend on the Holy Spirit and his work because they are engaging the secular world on its own turf. Too many sports minded people have no time for God and no place for church. Therefore, we should go to them and should rely on the Holy Spirit to begin his work in them. He is the One who will convict them of their sin. They think they are doing just fine, but the Spirit of God has his ways to convince them otherwise. Remember that without conviction of sin, there is no need for forgiveness and salvation. If you ever tried to impress a fairly good person of his need to have his sins forgiven, you know how difficult an assignment that can be. So why not trust the Holy Spirit with it? This work of convincing is his job anyway. He will do what is within his will and we can joyfully participate in it.

The Holy Spirit also convicts the world of righteousness. This righteousness is based on God's laws. We live in postmodern times where people do not accept God's absolutes as normative for them. They believe that everything is relative, depending on one's situation, therefore, righteousness does not originate with God, but with people who can determine what is right. Here is a major obstacle to our witness because of the collision of two widely different worldviews. The Holy Spirit knows our present situation better than we do and is capable to convince people of the higher ethical Christian behavior. He can reveal the righteousness of God that God the Father gave even before the coming of Christ. Christ simply lived that righteousness among us to show us the highest example for any human behavior. We should not be ashamed to propagate this righteousness of God.

Finally, the Holy Spirit convicts the world of judgment. I am always amused when unbelievers question God's power in regard to punishing evil. They have no idea what they are asking for. If God decided to judge all evil now, all people, who do not believe in Christ, would be immediately condemned to eternal death. The Bible is quite clear on this subject, "For all have sinned and fall short of the glory of God" (Romans 3:23). "For the wages of sin is death" (Romans 6:23). Since the judgment of unbelievers will be so complete, God is now offering mercy to all who would accept Jesus Christ as their Savior. Rather than asking for a swift judgment of God, now is the time when unbelievers should come to Christ to avoid their condemnation or they will join the prince of this world who is condemned already. He lost his battle with Christ who defeated death on the cross and returned to heaven. Yet, the final judgment is still before us. Revelation 14:7 records a warning, "Fear God and give him glory, because the hour of his judgment has come". Knowing about the coming judgment, we must spread the news whether people believe or not. Our proclamation coincides with the convincing work of the Holy Spirit to bring people to their senses and to avoid the judgment of God.

The Holy Spirit and our witness

Many Christians do not witness consistently about Christ because they are ignorant of the help of the Holy Spirit that is available. We are never alone during the proclamation of the Good news. It is of utmost importance to God that we present him to people; therefore, he is with us during our encounters with unbelievers.

First, the Holy Spirit works in the hearts of people before we talk to them. He arranges circumstances long before we get on the scene. Peter was hesitant to witness to the

Gentiles. He thought that the Gospel was just for the Jews. But the Holy Spirit was at work in the life of a Gentile by the name Cornelius. So he put in motion events that would bring these two men together. Peter had a vision of four-footed animals as well as reptiles coming down from heaven. Then he heard a voice telling him to kill those animals and to eat them. Peter objected because those animals were impure and unclean. But God insisted that nothing was impure that God has made clean. The vision vanished and Peter wondered what this meant. It did not take much time before the Spirit encouraged Peter to go with three men that would ask him to visit Cornelius to witness to him about Jesus.

The next day Peter started his journey to Caesarea where Cornelius, his relatives and close friends eagerly awaited what God would tell them through him. Peter first admitted that he had had some reservations about witnessing to the Gentiles, but he did not want to miss his opportunity because the Spirit of God was in it from the very beginning when he had a vision. Proclamation followed, and afterwards the Holy Spirit came on all who heard the message (Acts 10:1-48). We need more visions, more obedient witnesses, and more willing listeners.

I went on a mission trip to the Czech Republic. Many of the Czech people claimed to be atheists and did not want to talk to us. So I took my group to a local park, and we began to play sports with the young people there. Some of us played soccer, others played basketball, and yet others were throwing Frisbees. After a while we sat down to rest, and those youths tried to talk to us in English. This was an opportune time to share our testimonies with them and to explain the way of salvation. I asked them, "Do you understand what we shared with you?" They questioned us for about twenty minutes and then I challenged them to pray to receive Christ. At that moment, several of them left, but four remained. They expressed their desire to have their sins forgiven and to receive the gift of eternal life with God in heaven. After the prayer I asked every one of these 12 year olds, "Are your parents believers?" They answered in unison, "No, they are total atheists." There is no explanation for these conversions except for the work of the Holy Spirit that preceded our coming to the park.

Second, the Holy Spirit leads us to experience divine appointments. Do you remember what happened to Philip? He received instruction from the angel of the Lord to go to Gaza. There he met the Ethiopian eunuch. This time the further command came from the Holy Spirit saying that Philip should go to the chariot and stay near it. This event proved to be a divine appointment for Philip and the eunuch who later accepted Jesus and was baptized. The encouraging thing is that the Holy Spirit was not through with Philip. He took him away and transported him to Azotus for more witnessing encounters till he arrived to Caesarea (Acts 8:26-40). If we want to reach the world for Christ, we must allow the Holy Spirit to change our plans. I believe that the Holy Spirit wants to take us away from our comfortable places and use us in situations where people are ready to hear about Christ. There is a need for a word of caution. By presenting a positive example of Philip, the evangelist, I am not saying that every divine appointment will result in a conversion of a sinner. Sometime we have to keep on witnessing and leave the results in God's hands. Even Jesus, the Son of God, experienced rejection. And we do not know how Philip did in Caesarea where we meet him 20 years later (Acts 21:8). But we know one thing for sure that he was still Philip the evangelist. Faithfulness is the true mark of a witness.

Third, the Holy Spirit gives us power to witness. The parting words of Jesus Christ to his disciples promised power of the Holy Spirit in order to be witnesses to the ends of the earth (Acts 1:8). If a worldwide witness depended purely on us, it would be an impossible task. Many protestant denominations and organizations envisioned fulfilling the task of presenting the gospel to all nations by the end of the 20th century. It has not happened and there is no definite deadline on the horizon. We are more careful by giving a much more open goal like 2000 and beyond. Is it possible that we are failing in this area because we depend more on our great technological advances rather than on the power of the Holy Spirit? Computers, television and radio programs, videos, air travel, Bible translations, and all kinds of new methods should be employed, but the proclamation and winning people for Christ must be always done in the power of the Holy Spirit. The good fight of faith demands Christians who are filled with the Holy Spirit, not just those who have acquired the latest technological advances. We need to imitate the approach Paul took in planting a church in Thessalonica as he explained it in I Thess. 1:5, "because our gospel came to you not simply in words, but also with power, with the Holy Spirit and with deep conviction." As Paul proclaimed unashamedly the gospel, he knew that the power of God was present. He did not just speak words. Those words represented the power of God unto salvation of everyone who believed (Romans 1:16). But the Holy Spirit demonstrated his power in Paul's ministry also through signs and miracles (Romans 15:19). Effective witnesses manifest this kind of well rounded ministry.

Fourth, the Holy Spirit provides boldness. There is a great need in our post modern world to show boldness in proclaiming the only Savior of this world. Christians are forced by the public opinion and interest groups to retreat from claiming that Jesus Christ is the way and the truth and the life (John 14:6). Brittany McComb prepared her address to deliver it as the valedictorian at Foothill High School. She had to submit a copy of her speech to the school officials. They censored references to the Bible and Jesus Christ. Then they handed the corrected address over to the ACLU for approval. The ACLU approved the new version, but demanded no deviation from it. Brittany showed remarkable boldness in reading her original version. The school administrators caught on real fast and cut her mike before she could utter the name of Christ. The ACLU and the school administrators thought that they succeeded to silence another Christian. They were mistaken. Brittany and her parents appeared on Good Morning America and presented their case to the nation. Brittany said, "I went through four years of school at Foothill and they taught me logic and they taught me freedom of speech. God is the biggest part of my life. Just like other valedictorians thank their parents, I wanted to thank my Lord and Savior."[16]

Boldness for Christian witnesses is available from the Holy Spirit. The early disciples prayed for it and experienced the reality of true Christian courage, "Now, Lord consider their threats and enable your servants to speak your word with boldness. Stretch out your hand to heal and perform miraculous signs and wonders through the name of your holy servant Jesus. After they prayed, the place where they were meeting was shaken. And they were all filled with the Holy Spirit and spoke the word of God boldly" (Acts 4:29-31).

The ministry of the Holy Spirit is sufficient for our witness. A Christian who knows and desires the help of the Spirit of God, should not be ever afraid or timid in his witness. When we declare our complete dependence on the Holy Spirit, we will see results that will honor our Savior Jesus Christ.

THEOLOGICAL REFLECTIONS AND SPORTS EVANGELISM

Theology should not be relegated to theoretical thinking only. Knowing the mind of God concerning the evangelization of the world must produce innovating thinking and practice so that we make progress in achieving the goal set before us by Christ himself. The question before us is, "How can we improve our witness to secular people around us?" The major thesis of this book is that we must find a way to approach sports people with the gospel. They are all around us and most of them will not go to church on their own. They play or watch sports on Sunday. While we might gather one thousand believers in a sanctuary, there are more than one hundred thousands sports minded people in a stadium watching a car race and additional millions of fans sitting in front of their TV sets cheering their favorite drivers. There is no single verse in the Bible giving instructions about sports evangelism. So we need to look for a general principle that we could apply to our method.

Paul faced a similar problem. He was determined to fulfill the command of Christ to go and to carry the name of Christ "before the Gentiles and their kings and before the people of Israel" (Acts 9:15). His method was to use synagogues as the starting point to meet the Jews of a particular region. He presented the gospel among them and some of them became followers of Christ. But his assignment was much larger than just his countrymen. He had to reach the Gentiles and their kings. Visiting the local synagogue did not fit this enormous task. So he devised a new plan as we read about it in I Cor. 9:19-23, "Though I am free and belong to no man, I make myself a slave to everyone, to win as many as possible. To the Jews I became a Jew, to win the Jews. To those under the law I became like one under the law (though I myself am not under the law), so as to win those under the law. To those not having the law I became like one not having the law (though I am not free from God's law but am under Christ's law), so as to win those not having the law. To the weak I became weak, to win the weak. I have become all things to all men so that by all possible means I might save some. I do all this for the sake of the gospel, that I might share in its blessings."

Paul stated first that he was a free man. Nobody could force him to change his ways, however, he was under an obligation to preach the gospel unashamedly to all men. His freedom had to give way to the obedience of Christ. He realized that there were at least three groups of people the Jews, the Gentiles, and the weak who demanded adjustments in his life in order to gain them. Paul accepted this task at a great price. He had to become their slave. What a transformation from a free man to a slave. Patterson explained Paul's action as "an obsession with the commission that had been given to him."[17] Christ required it from Paul and is demanding it from us as well. There is no change in our status. We will not gain others for Christ, if we are not willing to go through this costly change.

In verse 22 Paul broadens his transformation to all things and to all men. Nobody is excluded so that all can be saved. There is an interesting change here from 'win' to 'save'. These words are synonymous in this context. Paul uses 'to win' five times and then he writes that he does all of this in order that he might save some. What does he mean? Paul certainly does not claim any power to save the lost. Patterson offers this interpretation, "The word 'save' always indicates the gravity of circumstances in which men are found. The circumstances are so serious that nothing short of a dramatic rescue can bring about their survival. Paul had access to the information that would lead men into that salvation. This had become the obsession of his life."[18]

We can follow Paul's example and establish a principle that would be biblical and practical. Notice those two inserted comments of Paul as he tries to qualify his statements about becoming like the Jews or the Gentiles. There were limits to resembling those he wanted to win. For instance, Paul circumcised Timothy (Acts 16:3) even though he knew that the ritual of circumcision was not valid for Christians. He did it for the sake of those Jews who lived Lystra. But if he was forced to go through this ritual for the sake of Timothy's salvation, he would certainly refuse to do it. In regard to those not having the law, Paul was voluntarily associating with them with the exception of upholding the law of Christ. The words of Maclaren will help us here, "The great principle incumbent on all Christians, with a view to the salvation of others, is to go as far as one can without untruthfulness in the direction of finding points of resemblance and contact with those to whom we would commend the Gospel."[19] We must determine at the very beginning how far we can go in assimilating ourselves to sports people. There is no question that they will ask us to accept their secular ways. They do not know any better. They think that their behavior is the norm. They live like that and they do not see much beauty in Christ and his followers. In fact, most of them think that Christians have very little fun in life.

I played professional ice hockey in Czechoslovakia. I gave it up during the Russian invasion in 1968 so that I could study for ministry. The Communistic government denied this privilege to me saying that I was more beneficial to the country playing ice hockey than preaching the gospel. I determined that it was more important to obey God than men and the inevitable happened. I left my home country on the sixth day of the invasion. My God provided a way out on August 26, and the next week I was accepted in the International Baptist Seminary in Ruschlikon, Switzerland. Since I also represented Czechoslovakia in tennis, I received a call in 1970 from a tennis coach from Oral Roberts University in Tulsa, Oklahoma. He offered me full scholarship for playing tennis, and I accepted. During summer months I played in professional tennis tournaments all over the States and Europe. I was also accepted into qualification rounds for French Open, Wimbledon, and the US Open. This was a great opportunity to be a witness among the best players in the world. I spoke with some of them about Christ and led a Bible study for others who were more interested. I am fully aware of the difficulties associated with becoming like those who need to hear the gospel, yet not giving up the Christian standard of living. It is like walking a tight rope. Alcohol, immorality, violence, lies, pretensions, and pride are ever present in the way of a witness. One wrong step and the fall is inevitable. Should this kind of danger keep us from getting involved? Paul would shout a resounding 'No'.

When my son learned to play ice hockey, we would go to play just for fun in an ice hockey stadium. One player noticed that we could help his team that played in an amateur league, so he invited us to join them. At the age of 62, I wondered whether that was a good idea. But my son wanted to play and I agreed to try it as well. We won the first game and the rest of the players invited us for a celebration which consisted of drinking quite a few bottles of beer. I do not drink, so I graciously declined. But they thought that my son, who was 19, would drink with them. You guessed it, he did not drink either. But we stayed and spoke with them about our lives and our relationship with Jesus Christ. They drank and listened. One of them told me later that they actually respected our decision not to drink. But there was another thing that made my sports evangelism difficult. I got hit by a stick that split my skin right below my nose. That is quite normal during an ice hockey game, but I did not enjoy driving to an emergency room to have three stitches put into a bleeding skin. Sports evangelism can be dangerous in more than one way, but the potential of reaching many people with the Good News is there.

Knowing the mind of God the Father, God the Son, and God the Holy Spirit should help us embrace the method of sports evangelism. It will open the doors into the hearts of people all over the world. The world wide sport of soccer is probably the best sport to use. Soccer is played in rich and poor countries. Every four years sixty four national soccer teams that qualified to play in the World Cup tournament will gather in one country to have a chance to become the world champion. Thousands upon thousands of fans will travel to that country to cheer their teams. And billions of fans will watch those matches on their TV screens in homes and in soccer stadiums scattered throughout the world. A sports evangelist needs only one soccer ball, the ability to kick it, and a desire to share Christ through this ministry. We can use other sports on a smaller scale while determining the best opportunity in a given country. The possibilities are enormous. It is up to Christians to do it.

CHAPTER FOUR

CHARACTERISTICS OF A SPORTS EVANGELISM WITNESS

The world of sports is not friendly to Christians. The majority of athletes and fans demand a clear demarcation line between sports and religion. They think religion might spoil the fun they have while playing or watching sports. This situation demands that we rethink who is capable to enter the scene. The sports evangelism witness has to exemplify certain characteristics that are not always demanded of other Christians. I realize that some of these marks will overlap, but others will be quite unique. Since we are dealing with the sports world, we are going to concentrate on the physical characteristics first.

PHYSICAL FITNESS

I am sure that you would question the presence of a professional golfer, or a baseball player who is visibly out of shape. Even if he is on the winning side, you still wonder why he is not taking care of his body. Any Christian, who would like to establish a relationship with an athlete, should try to manifest some physical fitness. If you think this demand is not biblical, listen to the words of III John 2, "Dear friend, I pray that you may enjoy good health and that all may go well with you, even as your soul is getting along well." Presently, good health is associated with proper weight and toned muscles. Aerobics is one sport that gained a lot of interest and publicity among those who want to live healthy lives. In order to find a listening ear among athletes, being in shape can help.

But there is another incentive for physical fitness. Paul writes, "Do you not know that your body is a temple of the Holy Spirit, who is in you, whom you have received from God? You are not your own; you were bought at a price. Therefore honor God with your body" (I Cor. 6:19). While reading the Book of Acts, the inescapable fact is that Paul was in a good physical shape. He walked and traveled constantly. He preached the Good News so tirelessly that even young people got tired and fell asleep (Acts 20:9). He persuaded Gentiles to believe on Jesus as he discussed his faith with them. He could not have done it without having a strong body because the mental abilities depend in part on physical fitness. He also knew enough about the athletic life to try to run and play sports. He did not just talk about honoring God through his body, he did it as well.

Our physical fitness is an integral part of our spiritual lives. We cannot live effective lives unless our bodies cooperate. There is no separation of body and spirit here. We cannot practice spiritual discipleship apart from our natural bodies. We cannot minister apart from engaging physically with other people. Our hands must offer a cup of cold water. Our feet have to walk to a place of need. Willard observes, "It is precisely this appropriate recognition of the body and of its implications for theology that is missing in currently dominant views of Christian salvation or deliverance. The human body is the focal point of human experience. Jesus had one. We have one. Without the body in its proper place, the pieces of the puzzle of new life in Christ do not realistically fit together, and the idea of really following him and becoming like him remains a practical impossibility."[1] This emphasis on the importance of our body functions as a corrective to our present day denial of paying attention to physical fitness. Do you know about any seminary that requires physical education courses? I went on many mission trips and so I know something about the physical preparedness of my students. Even though I challenged them to walk several miles a day to get ready for the mission trip, they did not take me seriously. Some of them had to stay in a hotel fairly early into the missionary activities because they couldn't keep up with the demands of prolonged walking up and down the city streets.

While practicing the spiritual discipline of evangelism, we must not overlook that part which our body plays. Evangelism demands physical exertion. A pastor walks many miles doing door-to-door witnessing. Servant evangelists need muscles to do acts of kindness. And sports evangelists sweat a lot playing sports with their friends. All of these activities make full use of the body. There is no place for Docetism here. In fact, Christ is known predominantly by bodily events of the incarnation, the crucifixion, and the resurrection. Paul makes a needed connection between us and Christ when he asks. "Do you not know that your bodies are members of Christ himself" (I Cor. 6:15)? Witnessing is not merely a spiritual event. Our bodies have dignity because of the presence of Christ in them. Willard adds, "The vitality and power of Christianity is lost when we fail to integrate our bodies into its practice by intelligent, conscious choice and steadfast intent."[2] But someone might object that the human body is portrayed in the Bible as 'lowly' (Philippians 3:21) and 'perishable' (I Cor. 15:50).

In some cases our bodies are a hindrance rather than help in evangelism. How do we resolve this paradox? The answer is in the fact that we have a choice when it comes to using our body. Paul claims that the perishable can be clothed with the imperishable (I Cor. 15:54). He also shows the way for the best choice when he writes in Romans 6:19, "Just as you used to offer the parts of your body in slavery to impurity and to ever-increasing wickedness, so now offer them in slavery to righteousness leading to holiness." We can manage our body so that we will not be hindered by it. Rather than complaining about being stuck in the body that responds to temptation, we can decide to do the will of God in this world.

Knowledge of postmodernism

Being athletic only, however, does not equip the evangelist to properly relate to sports people. The American culture has experienced a major shift from modernism to postmodernism. Even though some elements of modernism are not quite dead, we will pay attention to postmodernism which is more prevalent now and spreading throughout the world. The definition of postmodernism is elusive because of the nature of this cultural trend. So we will limit ourselves to ideas that describe it. Grassie observes:

> On the one hand, postmodernism and deconstruction are celebrated as the end of philosophical self-delusion, a critical attack on all oppressive metanarratives, and the final dissolution of foundational thought. On the other hand, postmodernism and deconstruction are denounced as relativistic, nihilistic, irrational, and hyper-rational. The inaccessible philosophic language of most postmodern thinkers and the heated confusion about what postmodernism represents make it difficult for the average professor teaching a science-and-religion class to acquire a working overview. And yet, at least a cursory understanding of these debates is essential to any discussion of science and religion in the late twentieth century.[3]

There is no reason for us not to know how to respond to the changing scene of our culture. If we do not have a general idea of postmodernism, we will approach sports minded people in a way that will not be effective.

McRaney provides helpful starting points for conversations within modernity and postmodernity contexts:

Modernity	Postmodernity
Heaven or hell	Significance, meaning, purpose
The Bible	Life issues
Our agenda	Their situation
Universal truths (death, taxes)	Personal examples
"Nice to meet you"	"Because we are friends, I…"
Confrontational	Relational
Church or religious topics/experiences	Spiritual topics and experiences
"How do you stand with God?"	"Describe your spiritual journey."
Jesus	God
Giving information	Asking inquiring questions
Having the right words	Living the right way
John 3:16; Romans 3:23	Genesis 1:1; Jeremiah 28:11
Gospel facts	Gospel's impact and testimony[4]

The shift from modernity to postmodernity is built on the premise that everything is relative and that there is no objective truth that all people can embrace. If this is true, then all we can do is to share our experiences. Therefore, people are open to discussing purpose in life, meaning of human existence, relationships, life issues, and especially personal opinions on how things work for them. We can no longer count on knowledge of biblical facts. Postmodern people do not know them, and if they are aware of some of them, they do not accept them. The usual answer goes like this, "The Bible is just another book so do not quote verses out of it for me." Rather than starting with the propositional truth as we know it from God's word, we should make full use of sharing our testimony because nobody can argue that it is not true. However, we cannot count on our shared experience alone to convince them of the truthfulness of Christianity. They will admit that faith in Jesus works for us, but there is not always willingness on their part to think it will work for them as well. Because of this postmodern mindset, we should think about sports evangelism as a process. It begins with building a relationship. As we become friends, we can speak about Christ and what he means to us. Then we have to demonstrate the beauty of the Christian life in daily encounters and pray for an open heart to accept Christ.

While we communicate with the secular people, we must anticipate their questions. It should not be extremely difficult because those questions are directly connected with the starting point of our conversations. Here is a sample of the gradual change of questions in our time as McRaney sees them:

Modernity	Postmodernity
Is Christianity rational?	Do you care about me?
How do I know there is a God?	What is my purpose in life?
Are miracles possible?	Is there ultimate meaning?
Do science and Scripture conflict?	How can I experience God?
Are Christianity's claims valid?	How can I become God/ get right with God?
Why does God allow suffering and evil?	Is Jesus the only way to God?
What are the essentials of the gospel?	Are gospel essentials real? (Do they make a difference)
Is it worth the sacrifice to follow Christ?	Integrity – does it work?
Has no one told them about Jesus?	Which god?
Is the Bible trustworthy?	What can God do for me?
Evolution – (Bible versus science)	Which religion is right for me?
Gospel facts	Which holy book is right?
Not enough answers to questions	No one has shown them Jesus
Existence of God	Poor image of the church
Can't explain God	Lack of credibility of Christians
Suffering in the world	Not enough mystery of God
Bible versus science	Make sense of life, TV, virtual reality
Darwinism	Make order/meaning out of chaos
	Exclusivity of Christ in the midst of pluralism
	Terminology/understanding a message
	Looking for hope
	Bible versus experience
	Connecting with God[5]

The questions listed above show the disillusionment of postmodern people. They have no real answers to the basic questions of humanity, yet they are not willing to accept the eternal God revealed in Jesus Christ. The idealistic promises of modern philosophers concerning humanistic ethics, scientific progress, and human capabilities to solve societal problems have proved to be empty words. What is left for people without God? Their spiritual restlessness drives them to spirituality that dethrones reason and offers intuitive feelings and a way to self elevation. They live for the present moment filled with temporal, pleasurable experiences. Christians should not be timid about reaching out to these people. Knowing about their disillusionment, we can knock down the idols of postmodernity. But our approach will demand integrity of Christian lives that cannot be manufactured by secular people. Living in a pagan society should give us a great advantage in showing the difference of life lived with the help of the Holy Spirit as compared with the self-centered life of a person who has no hope beyond this life.

SPIRITUAL FITNESS

Doing the work of the Lord in the world presupposes physical and spiritual fitness. As much as we have to keep our bodies in shape, the more we need to make sure that our spiritual fitness is not lagging behind. Unless we keep on growing spiritually, we will get exhausted and will give up the good fight of faith.

Conversion. The very beginning of the spiritual life happens when one is born again. This is the divine origin of becoming a child of God. The words of Jesus Christ to Nicodemus shed light on this subject, "I tell you the truth, no one can enter the kingdom of God unless he is born of water and Spirit. Flesh gives birth to flesh, but Spirit gives birth to spirit. You should not be surprised at my saying, 'You must be born again.'" (John 3:5-7). God guarantees this beginning through faith in Jesus Christ. John assures us that, "He who has the Son has life; he who does not have the Son of God does not have life. I write these things to you who believe on the name of the Son of God so that you may know that you have eternal life" (I John 5:12-13). The assurance of the eternal life in Christ plays a vital role in the progression to spiritual maturity and in the capability to present Christ to others.

Being filled with the Holy Spirit. We have already established the fact that we cannot evangelize in our own strength. Only the Holy Spirit can bring people to the saving knowledge of Jesus Christ and so provide for the new birth.

But the Holy Spirit is using Christians to proclaim the gospel; therefore, we must be fully under the control of the Spirit of God. Paul states a clear command in Ephesians 5:18, "Do not get drunk on wine, which leads to debauchery. Instead, be filled with the Spirit." The illustration is readily understood. Drunkards are behaving under the influence of alcohol. They do things they would not usually do. Their mental abilities are changed depending on the level of alcohol in their blood. Paul warns us not to be drunk on wine. He knows about a better option that is beneficial to all Christians at all times. Being filled with the Spirit, or being under the control of the Spirit, is the only way we can effectively evangelize.

In order that we fulfill this condition, we must understand that the infilling of the Spirit of God is not a static phenomenon. The initial filling happens at the moment of faith in Jesus Christ (Acts 15: 8-9). But what follows are subsequent fillings. If it were not so, then the disciples would not have been filled with the Spirit again and again (Acts 2:4; 4:8, 31; 9:17; 13:9). We are not any better than the first disciples of Christ. We are capable of grieving the Holy Spirit (Ephesians 4:30). We can put out the Spirit's fire (I Thess. 5:19). So the infilling of the Spirit fluctuates due to sin in our lives, and we had better be open to the subsequent fillings in order to satisfy the command of God upon us. How can it be done?

The starting point is an honest confession of sins. John tells us that, "If we confess our sins, he is faithful and just and will forgive us our sins and purify us from all unrighteousness" (I John 1:9). Confession will result in a pure heart where the Holy Spirit can fully reside. Then it is important to submit to the Spirit of God unreservedly. Every area of life must be surrendered to him. No locked closets. No unholy desire. Everything has to be seen from the perspective of the Holy Spirit whose task it is to bring glory to Jesus Christ (John 16:14). Once you take these steps of true discipleship, you can be sure that the Holy Spirit is in charge of your life filling you with his presence and power. You can experience the fulfillment of the promise of Christ to his disciples before returning to his Father, "But you will receive power when the Holy Spirit comes on you; and you will be my witnesses in Jerusalem, and in all Judea and Samaria, and to the ends of the earth" (Acts 1:8).

Obedience. A disciple knows Christ's will and obediently puts it into practice. Quite simple, isn't it? Not so! To follow Christ obediently presents many challenges to our own understanding of what we want to do. The rich young ruler kept many commandments. Even Jesus was impressed by his life. But then Jesus asked him to sell his possessions and give to the poor if he wanted to be perfect. This young man had to obey to do just one thing to achieve perfection and to follow Jesus. Did he obey? The Bible gives an answer, "When the young man heard this, he went away sad, because he had great wealth" (Matt. 19:22). Bonhoeffer shows a penetrating insight concerning the relationship of faith and obedience, "The idea of a situation in which faith is possible is only a way of stating the facts of a case in which the following two propositions hold good and are equally true: *only he who believes is obedient, and only he who is obedient believes.*"[6]

Obedience is intrinsically interwoven with faith. Faith in Christ does not shrink from his commands. If it does, it becomes an expression of cheap grace rather than the costly grace that Christ offered to us. Yet we are tempted to refuse the cost of discipleship while rationalizing our disobedience for the sake of comfort and convenience. Our world is not, however, impressed by this sort of Christianity. Bonhoeffer explains this dilemma,

> In the modern world it seems so difficult to walk with absolute certainty in the narrow way of ecclesiastical decision and yet remain in the broad open spaces of the universal love of Christ, of the patience, mercy and 'philanthropy' of God (Titus 3:4) for the weak and the

> ungodly. Yet somehow or other we must combine the two, or else we shall follow the paths of men. May God grant us joy as we strive earnestly to follow the way of discipleship. May we be enabled to say 'No' to sin and 'Yes' to the sinner. May we withstand our foes, and yet hold out to them the Word of the gospel which woos and wins the souls of men.[7]

There are many aspects of obedience, but we shall mention the one which is the main theme of this book. We must be obedient in finding a way to reach the ungodly in stadiums and sports fields in our world. The command is inescapable and demands action.

Holiness. Probably the most difficult part of spiritual fitness is the call to holiness (I Cor. 1:2). Paul repeats this call as he writes his second letter to Timothy 1:8-9, "So do not be ashamed to testify about our Lord, or ashamed of me his prisoner. But join with me in suffering for the gospel, by the power of God, who has saved us and called us to a holy life – not because of anything we have done but because of his own purpose and grace." We are to be separated unto God as we live holy lives for him. The difficulty is in the fact that we live in a world that presents many temptations to those who are to be holy. We have to reject certain sinful actions and yet stay in touch with secular people who need God. A constant battle rages on. Paul describes it in Romans 8:37-39, "No, in all these things we are more than conquerors through him who loved us. For I am convinced that neither death nor life, neither angels nor demons, neither the present nor the future, nor any powers, neither height nor depth, nor anything else in all creation, will be able to separate us from the love of God that is in Christ Jesus our Lord." Yes, we are more than conquerors, but that does not mean we are handed victories on a silver platter without any effort. Willard explains, "Once the individual has through divine initiative become alive to God and his Kingdom, the extent of integration of his or her total being into that Kingdom order significantly depends upon the individual's initiative.....we also learn by experience that the harmonization of our total self with God will not be done for us. We must act."[8]

The great majority of Christians think that the regular church attendance is a sign of holy living even though it is limited to Sunday and possibly to Wednesday. Others go a little bit further by insisting on performing different religious duties like tithing, serving on committees, teaching in Sunday School and so on. But these activities do not guarantee holiness because they are limited to the religious scene. A better way is to practice spiritual disciplines. Willard defines spiritual disciplines as, "activities of mind and body purposefully undertaken to bring our personality and total being into effective cooperation with the divine order."[9] There is no complete, authoritative list of disciplines in spite of many works written on this subject. Willard claims to have listed those disciplines that have been practiced and profitable for Christians of differing backgrounds. Here they are:

Disciplines of Abstinence

Solitude

Silence

Fasting

Frugality

Chastity

Secrecy

Sacrifice

Disciplines of Engagement

Study

Worship

Celebration

Service

Prayer

Fellowship

Confession

Submission[10]

Richard Foster divides his list into three parts:

The Inward Disciplines

Meditation

Prayer

Fasting

Study

The Outward Disciplines

Simplicity

Solitude

Submission

Service

The Corporate Disciplines

Confession

Worship

Guidance

Celebration[11]

We will not extrapolate each of these disciplines. The list is for those who would like to deepen their spirituality through the practice of these disciplines. Willard's and Foster's lists do not include the discipline of evangelism that is pertinent to our study. But they would not object to our addition because they do not claim to have lists of all possible disciplines.[12] Donald Whitney introduces the discipline of evangelism and justifies his choice, "But evangelism is also a *Discipline* in that we must discipline ourselves to get into the context of evangelism, that is, we must not just wait for witnessing opportunities to happen."[13] An undisciplined Christian will admit that witnessing for Christ is his duty, but he will not get around to doing it. He will not put himself in a situation where proclaiming the Good News is possible. He will not use his time wisely. He will not pray for the lost by name. He will not train himself to share the gospel. He will subconsciously hope for the ideal encounter that never happens. Yes, evangelism is a spiritual discipline.

The secret of the effective Christian is in a disciplined life that knows no spiritual vacation. We must not limit our holiness to one day a week. God calls us to holiness that is always visible and demonstrable in the world. Paul sums it up in Romans 6:13, "Do not offer the parts of your body to sin, as instruments of wickedness, but rather offer yourselves to God, as those who have been brought from death to life; and offer the parts of your body to him as instruments of righteousness." Holiness is achievable through the process of sanctification that goes on throughout our Christian lives. There are no shortcuts as Francis de Sales explains,

> The ordinary purification and healing, whether of the body or of the mind, takes place only little by little, by passing from one degree to another with labor and patience. The angels upon Jacob's ladder had wings; yet they flew not, but ascended and descended in order from one step to another. The soul that rises from sin to devotion may be compared to the dawning of the day, which at its approach does not expel darkness instantaneously but little by little.[14]

There is no possibility of an instant holiness. The transformation of a Christian goes on and on as he participates with God in this process. Nobody should despair of this slow progression. We are running a race and fighting the good fight of faith. Through it all God is on our side encouraging us to be set apart for him.

Ability to communicate the gospel. We have already written about our ever changing society from modernity to postmodernity. Erickson even writes about a need to address what he calls postpostmodernity, "What I am proposing is that evangelicals need to be in the vanguard of thought. Rather than merely relating to postmodernism, evangelicals must understand that postmodernism is simply another stop along the way, not the final destination. We must be preparing for the postpostmodern era, and even helping to bring it about, while realizing that it, or actually probably several varieties of postpostmodern life and thought, will not be the terminus of the process either."[15] No matter what the name of the future era will be, one thing is for sure that there is no slowing down of the frantic changes around us. Evangelicals are not always ready to embrace change for the sake of communicating the gospel. Our church buildings are sanctuaries where things can go on without modifying our ways. But when we enter the secular world on Sunday afternoon, we are brutally shocked by our inability to communicate with the postmodern people. Some Christians think they can use the same language inside and outside our churches. They even think that the pagans around them should understand the King James Version of the Bible as they quote verses to them. But language and culture change as time goes on, and we must make adjustments if we want to make sense sharing Christ with the people around us.

In the 1950s we could presume that people in America had a positive attitude toward Christianity. They were able to identify the gospel writers and had some idea about the basic facts in the gospels. More than 50 years later the situation is vastly different. James Engel and William Dyrness developed a figure of the spiritual decision process in the year 2000:

Spiritual reproduction

ACTIVATION

Incorporation in church

FOLLOW UP

Reevaluation

HARVESTING

Change of allegiance

Problem recognition

Positive attitude toward becoming Christian

SEED SOWING &
WATERING

Understanding of gospel implications

Knowledge of gospel basics

No awareness[16]

Reading this table from bottom to top will reveal that nowadays we face people who have no awareness of a Supreme Being or who categorically deny his existence. We cannot begin speaking with these pagans by quoting John 3:16 to them, even though it is the greatest news, for the simple reason that they do not believe in the existence of a God who loves them. If they believe that humans evolved from lower species, we must engage them in a conversation of the possibility of an intelligent design that demands a Creator. This is not as difficult as it seems. Atheists are not quite convinced of their atheism. They have no scientific facts to back up their belief. And if they are willing to think logically about our universe, they will allow us to talk to them about our God who revealed himself to us through his Son Jesus Christ. At this point we can introduce our experience with God who has changed our lives. You remember that the postmodern people are impressed with the reality of a personal experience.

I witnessed to enough atheists in the Czech Republic where I was able to poke holes in their unscientific belief in evolution. Some of them were surprised to learn that evolution was not science, but a theory. They were victims of a lie repeated so many times that it became the unquestionable truth for them. It was interesting to me to see their attention rise and to be able to answer questions about the other possibility: "Who is your God? How come you can actually know him?" I laid a groundwork that enabled me to continue my witness. But if I started delivering a gospel outline devised in the past century, they would have turned me off in a hurry. We need a spirit of discernment in order to start spiritual conversations at the place where the particular person finds himself.

Those who have some knowledge of the basics of the gospel do not necessarily want to accept them for themselves. Usually they know that Christ was born, lived on this earth, died on the cross, and supposedly rose from the dead. To these facts they say, "So what? There are many stories out there from different world religions and there must be some truth in all of them." These are the indifferent people who want no commitment. They think that they have the right to develop their own set of beliefs, especially those that suit their lifestyle.

Understanding of gospel implications falls into the sphere of seed sowing and watering. People who hear the gospel will either consider it seriously, or will tend to reject it. There is no middle ground. Christ demands all or nothing. He brought the ultimate sacrifice for the salvation of those who believe and so his requirements are justly all encompassing. Engel and Dyrness rightly place this group of people among those who must be considered with patience and love. We must be available so that the Holy Spirit would use our witness to convince them of sin, righteousness, and judgment. This process is within the power of the Spirit of God. We are merely instruments who can proclaim the gospel and wait upon God. Is there a specific way we should present the gospel to sports minded people? There is a theme in the Bible that can appeal to athletes. Every athlete, amateur or professional, wants to win. The idea of being victorious is prevalent in the New Testament writings. Athletes understand existentially the difference between defeat and victory better than any other group of people.

In order to make full use of this method, we have to learn how to converse. Pippert suggests a conversational model that is helpful. She presents three steps: "investigate, stimulate, relate."[17] Asking questions is an appropriate way of investigating. This should not become mechanical just to keep the conversation going. Rather, we should be genuinely interested in the person with whom we are communicating. There is a need for a special skill that we can develop by asking interesting questions that reveal our curiosity. Then we should simply listen and process the clues we are hearing. We might not be right every time as to our interpretation, but people usually do not mind sharing with someone who shows concern. Questions that relate to sports evangelism are: "What is your favorite sport? Does your family enjoy playing with you? Do you win often, or do you compete just for fun? How do you handle defeat? What do you do to win? Where do you keep your trophies? Would you like to know about a trophy that is valuable throughout eternity? Would you like to know how to gain this trophy?" All these questions can actually stimulate people to hear how the gospel answers them. Pippert observes, "We try to saturate people with information before we have caught their attention." [18]If we want to speak about the victorious life through Christ, we must figure out whether people even want to know what is involved.

When Jesus talked with the Samaritan woman, he aroused her interest by offering her the living water (John 4:10). She questioned his ability to do so, but kept on conversing with Jesus. Then she asked for that water. Surprisingly, Jesus changed the topic of their conversation. Instead of explaining what he was talking about, he told her to bring her husband to him. Why would he do that? She was not ready for the whole message. She needed more stimulation of her curiosity. Little warns:

> Give people only as much of the message as they are ready for, don't condemn them….The moment we detect a faint glimmer of interest in non-Christians, many of us want

> to rush right in and rattle off the whole gospel without coming up for air or waiting for any audience response. (After all, we might not get another chance, we think!) But by relying on the power and presence of the Holy Spirit, we can gain poise. Non-Christians need gentle coaxing when they're just beginning to show interest: it's usually fragile at first. Otherwise, like birds scared from their perches by a sudden movement toward them, they will withdraw. On the other hand, if we are casual in our attitude and relaxed in our manner, the inquirers might even press us to share with them."[19]

I exercised this caution especially with athletes who did not live moral lives. I could have told them outright that God would not tolerate their sinful ways. Their response would be, "Well, I do not want to have anything with your God." A better approach was to continue the relationship and to exemplify a holy life. In fact, I saw the wisdom of this approach in my relationship with ice hockey players on my team in the 1960s. Some of them seemingly did not pay attention to me and my witness. But when I met two of them during my visit to the Czech Republic in 2003, I began to witness to them again. I did investigating and stimulating which are pre-evangelism activities. The third step had to follow, whether immediately or after some time. I had to depend on the Holy Spirit to lead me. It was the right time to relate the basics of the gospel. My fellow ice hockey players responded to my proclamation, "We also believe in Jesus." They must have seen something good in the way I lived and witnessed among them.

If the introductory questions led into a positive conversation, you can quote I Cor. 9:24-25, "Do you not know that in a race all the runners run, but only one gets the prize? Run in such a way as to get the prize. Everyone who competes in the games goes into strict training. They do it to get a crown that will not last; but we do it to get a crown that will last forever." Paul used a vivid illustration from his experience of the Isthmian games that occurred every two years. He pointed out that the runner received a perishable wreath that was woven out of laurel leaves. The wreath was placed on the head of the winner who enjoyed it for a time, but eventually it would wither. The victory itself was recorded, but could not be repeated by the same runner when he got old. The ability to run fast vanished. In the same way, our trophies and accomplishments have only a temporal value. Pointing people to the imperishable crown then makes a lot of sense.

So far we established a common ground. We conversed and agreed on some things we deemed important. But now we have to make a major switch. We want to lead these people to God with the intention to explain to them what it takes for them to find real and eternal purpose for life through faith in God. We want to participate in the work of the Holy Spirit in their lives; therefore, we must understand what is involved. Michael Green uses the conversion experience of the apostle Paul to show four aspects of this tremendous event:

> God touched his conscience
>
> God touched his mind
>
> God touched his will
>
> God transformed the whole of the rest of his life.[20]

Paul's conversion was unique, yet he wrote to Timothy, "But for that very reason I was shown mercy so that in me, the worst of sinners, Christ Jesus might display his unlimited patience as an example for those who would believe on him and receive eternal life" (I Tim. 1:16). It is legitimate for us to draw principles out of Paul's conversion for our own conclusions. When we witness, we must present the whole gospel, depending on the circumstances, and stress the need for a complete transformation that touches the conscience, the mind, and the will not just for that particular moment of decision for Christ, but for the rest of life. Paul's conscience was pricked when Jesus asked him, "Saul, Saul, why do you persecute me" (Acts 9:4)? At that point Paul knew he was a sinner. He had a need of a Savior. Only Jesus could forgive his sins. Next, Paul had to change his mind on some preconceived ideas. He could not believe in a Messiah who ended up on the cross. He was determined to persecute those who believed in this accursed Messiah.

The Old Testament stated clearly that anyone who was hung on a tree was under God's curse (Deut. 21:23). The change in Paul's thinking occurred when Paul understood that Christ became accursed while bearing our curse, "Christ redeemed us from the curse of the law by becoming a curse for us" (Gal. 3:13). Paul also changed his mind about the resurrection of Christ. He met the living Christ on the way to Damascus. He spoke with him. He received a lifelong assignment from him and he accepted this task in spite of the fact that suffering was an integral part of it. The surprising thing was that Paul did not receive a contract with a detailed description of his missionary trips and yet he signed up without any hesitation. Finally, Paul determined freely that this would be the way to live, "Saul spent several days with the disciples in Damascus. At once he began to preach in the synagogues that Jesus is the Son of God. All those who heard him were astonished and asked, "Isn't he the man who raised havoc in Jerusalem among those who call on this name? And hasn't he come here to take them as prisoners to the chief priests?" Yet Saul grew more and more powerful and baffled the Jews living in Damascus by proving that Jesus is the Christ (Acts 19:22).

Luke did not include any description of Paul's emotions during his conversion experience. Paul probably did not share those details with him to write them down. We will not try to speculate. Some emotions are definitely expressed when people receive Christ as their Savior, but they are not normative for that experience. What is ultimately important is the transformation of the whole being that lasts throughout the life of a Christian. No conversion is for real when it is limited just to a single moment at the end of an emotionally charged evangelistic service. If that decision is recorded in the Book of Life, then the new believer will remain faithful to Christ for the rest of his life. Green quotes Leo Tolstoy as he describes his conversion:

> Five years ago I came to believe in Christ's teaching, and my life suddenly changed. I ceased to desire what I previously desired, and began to desire what I formerly did not

> want. What had previously seemed to me good seemed evil, and what had seemed evil seemed good. It happened to me as it happens to a man who goes out on some business, and on the way decides that the business is unnecessary and returns home. All that was on his right is now on his left, and all that was on his left in now on his right.[21]

In our postmodern culture, we are tempted to lessen the demands of Christ upon the lives of those who want to follow him. It is necessary to present the gospel that is not watered down in any way. That is the only gospel the Holy Spirit will use. Our emphasis on the victorious Christian life must not overshadow the essentials of the gospel.

GOSPEL PRESENTATION

What are the basics of the gospel proclamation? Many evangelistic tracts summarize the gospel in four steps. The most popular are the Four Spiritual Laws of the Campus Crusade and Steps to Peace with God published by Billy Graham Evangelistic Association. These tracts presuppose that people believe in God. As we already mentioned, it is no longer true about all people in the postmodern world;

therefore, we must begin with the proclamation of God who created our universe.

Step one: God created you, loves you, and wants you to be a winner. "In the beginning God created the heavens and the earth" (Genesis 1:1). This is our belief that is based on the word of God. Hopefully, we have already laid a foundation for this statement because without it we cannot move on with the postmodern people. But the Christian belief deals with more than just a God who is removed from us and who simply set the Universe in motion and does not interfere with human affairs.

We believe in the God who loves all people, "For God so loved the world that he gave his one and only Son, that whoever believes in him shall not perish but have eternal life" (John 3:16). God proved his love for us by sending his Son to live among us, completing his work of salvation on the cross, rising from the dead on the third day, and finally ascending to the heavens to be with his Father. Now Jesus shows his love for us by being actively involved in our lives, as Paul puts it in Romans 8:33-34, "Who will bring any charge against those whom God has chosen? It is God who justifies. Who is he who condemns? Christ Jesus, who died – more than that, who was raised to life – is at the right hand of God and is also interceding for us."

With Jesus on our side, we can live victorious lives. John was fully convinced of it when he wrote these words, "[for] everyone born of God overcomes the world. This is the victory that has overcome the world, even our faith. Who is it that overcomes the world? Only he who believes that Jesus is the Son of God" (I John 5:4-5). We can be sure of the final victory. This is a fact that no athlete can claim. There is always some doubt about the next race, match, or game. Things can go wrong at any time. Athletes can get hurt. They pull a muscle. They get thrown against the boards. They can crash their cars. The referee can make a bad call and ruin the rest of the game. Finally, time claims even the superstar athletes and victories are not there anymore. The wise athletes, like John Elway or Wayne Gretzky, retired before they would become losers. Many other athletes just cannot leave the sports scene and start losing or join a senior league where they compete on a lower level. But even they will eventually realize they can no longer win.

John is talking about the victory that is physical, mental, and spiritual. It is a known fact that our bodies function better when we cherish a legitimate hope. While we live here on earth, we make sure that we do not mistreat our body because the physical body is the temple of the Holy Spirit. We make progress toward experiencing the imperishable body that is glorious, and powerful (I Cor. 15:42-43). Mentally, we succeed controlling our minds by following Paul's instruction, "Finally, brothers, whatever is true, whatever is noble, whatever is right, whatever is pure, whatever is lovely, whatever is admirable – if anything is excellent or praiseworthy – think about such things. Whatever you have learned or received or heard from me, or seen in me – put it into practice. And the God of peace will be with you" (Phil. 4:8-9). The real victory, especially in our torn up world, is having the peace of God that transcends all understanding. This is the peace that stems from the determination to live for God according to his purpose for our lives. When we decide to live a life committed to God, then we live the abundant life that is not limited to our physical, athletic capabilities, "I have come that they may have life, and have it to the full" (John 10:10a).

The final victory is placed into the spiritual realm of the Kingdom of God. Paul claims that death does not have the last word, "Where, O death is your victory? Where, O death is your sting?" The sting of death is sin, and the power of sin is the law. But thanks be to God! He gives us the victory through our Lord Jesus Christ. Therefore, my dear brothers, stand firm. Let nothing move you. Always give yourselves fully to the work of the Lord, because you know that your labor in the Lord is not in vain" (I Cor. 15:55-58). We already taste some of this victory through our relationship with Christ, but the full extent of it is still before us. Since we are so sure of it, we can live constructive lives of serving God and the people around us. Why is it that not all people are experiencing the life that God truly desires for them? The prophet Isaiah explains, "But your iniquities have separated you from your God; your sins have hidden his face from you, so that he will not hear" (Isaiah 59:2).

Step two. The gravest problem of all people is sin. Sin is experienced universally. Nobody is exempted. Romans 3:23 states poignantly, "[for] all have sinned and fall short of the glory of God." Sin causes trouble, unhappiness, deceit, disruption, alienation, suffering, and horror. We do not have to teach people to sin. All of us are capable of sinning early in our lives. The evidences of sin are all around us. So why is it that since the address of President Eisenhower in 1953 no American president has mentioned sin as a national failure? Sin is not a popular word. It reminds us of missing the mark that God placed before us.

Karl Menninger wrote a book he entitled *Whatever Became of Sin?* In it, he finds Webster's definition of sin incomplete because, "it fails to say why the transgression and disobedience are regarded as "bad," why they are popularly disapproved or forbidden, considered to be "No, no." Sin traditionally does have this quality of taboo, of wrongness, and we can assume it is carried over from the earliest days. The wrongness of the sinful act lies not merely in its nonconformity, its departure from the accepted, appropriate way of behavior, but in an implicitly aggressive quality – a ruthlessness, a hurting, a breaking away from God and from the rest of humanity, a partial alienation, or act of rebellion."[22] Menninger gets help from Hiltner in defining sin from the Christian theological perspective, "as *rebellion;* as *estrangement* or *isolation;* and as *error* in performance, a missing of the mark (the old Hebrew meaning)."[23] None of these actions show man in a favorable light. No wonder that the postmodern man rejects the concept of sin and so tries to avoid any thought of guilt, accountability, and responsibility for his actions. According to Menninger, "Sins had become crimes and now crimes were becoming illnesses; in other words whereas the police and judges had taken over from clergy, the doctors and psychologists were now taking over from police and judges."[24] The new psychologists seem to have the upper hand in defining wrong behavior. They have succeeded in taking sin from public view and so desensitized the conscience of the postmodern man.

I experienced this fact in my ministry when I organized a tennis clinic on the property of Hulen Street Baptist Church. I secured the help of the best tennis instructors in Fort Worth, Texas and then I publicized the clinic for over two months in the local newspaper. 450 students showed up on Saturday morning to receive tennis instruction. We spent three hours on the tennis courts playing and interacting with our students. Everybody seemed to enjoy the clinic. At the end I thanked the tennis professionals for their presence and effort to give those people important tips to improve their game. Then I said to the players, "We gave you a free tennis lesson, now I would like to invite you into our sanctuary to hear about the free offer of salvation in Jesus Christ. You are not obligated in any way to stay because the clinic is over. But if you are interested to hear what we have to say about Christ, you are welcome to stay."

About 420 people filled the sanctuary. I am sure that many of those people were Christians, but some needed to hear the gospel. So I proceeded to explain the way of salvation and the possibility of eternal life with God through faith in Jesus Christ. Six people came forward to learn more about becoming Christians. Our counselors talked with them and answered their questions. We felt their decisions were genuine and so we encouraged them to go to church where they lived and to profess their faith there.

The clinic happened on Saturday and on Monday I had a visitor in my office. He introduced himself as the father of a 12 year old boy who participated in our clinic and who wanted to become a Christian. Then he began shouting at me and threatening me, "How dare you talk to my son about his need to have his sins forgiven? You had no right to tell him that."

I answered, "It is the ministry of this church to tell people about this wonderful offer to have their sins forgiven through faith in Jesus Christ. It is consistent with the Christian message of salvation. You should have known that your son was going to a Baptist Church to play tennis. Our advertisements in the Fort Worth Star Telegram clearly stated that it was an event where we would teach tennis on the courts of the Hulen Street Baptist Church. We did nothing that would be inconsistent with our Christian witness and with our concern that all people would hear about Jesus.

He countered, "My son is no sinner." "Is that so?" I asked, "Tell me how many times your son lied to you?" He did not answer that question, but volunteered to tell me that his Methodist pastor does not preach about sin. Then he changed his tactic by trying to make me afraid, "I will make you life miserable in this town," he went on, "and I will write letters to different institutions and tell them what you are doing here."

I replied, "I will be glad when you publicize what I do in this church." That remark made him even angrier. He was just about ready to hit me. Instead, he walked out of my office and slammed the door so hard that I thought it would collapse the whole wall. At that point I appreciated my former experiences as an ice hockey player. I stood my ground and was bold, by the grace of God, in my witness.

The popular leaning is away from addressing the problem of sin head on. It is a shame that even some clergy have given up preaching on the sinfulness of man. Convincing people of their sin is essential to witnessing. If they do not admit that they are sinners, then they have no need of a Savior. I actually witnessed to a man who stated categorically, "You have no right to call me a sinner!" His definition of sin included only a murder. The rest of his behavior was exempted from the idea of being a sinner. I knew him fairly well and I was aware of his immoral escapades that were causing him much trouble. But he would not budge. I met him two years later when he went through a bitter divorce. Only then he admitted that he had a problem that could be defined as sin. He begged me to help him. "I am in search of faith," he claimed. I spent more than two hours answering his questions that he would not have asked in the past. He did not receive Christ that day, but he was willing to know more about him and his offer of forgiveness.

If we do not describe sin in its ugliness, who will? Menninger laments:

> We know that the principal leadership in the morality realm should be the clergy's, but they seem to minimize their great traditional and historical opportunity to preach, to prophesy, to speak out. Spiritual leadership must indeed have intelligent following, so where are the lawyers, teachers, editors, publishers, and others to take up the lead?
>
> Some clergymen prefer pastoral counseling of individuals to the pulpit function. But the latter is a greater opportunity to both heal *and prevent*. An ounce of prevention is worth a pound of cure, indeed, and there is much prevention to be done for large numbers of people who hunger and thirst after direction toward righteousness. Clergymen have a golden opportunity to prevent some of the accumulated misapprehensions, guilt, aggressive action, and the other roots of later mental suffering and mental disease.[25]

In this statement, Menninger exercises his right to ask the clergy to preach and to prophesy, however, this task is not limited just to the clergy. Peter writes that all Christians are a royal priesthood (I Peter 2:9). Luther is known for his emphasis on the priesthood of all believers. Priests are to introduce people to God by facilitating worship. This is a tremendous responsibility that must be done biblically. Nobody can come into the presence of God to worship him and to know him without dealing with sin. We do a great disservice to seekers, if we are afraid to tell them what God thinks of their sins. Keeping from them the call to repentance will prevent them from becoming true Christians. They will be nominal Christians who do not have a saving faith. The truth of the matter is that too many members of our churches belong to this group. The faulty presentation of the essentials of faith in Christ is the reason for nominal Christians who are not different from secular people. Understanding the gravity of sin as described in Romans 6:23, "For the wages of sin is death," can serve as a proper correction for our proclamation. God will punish all sin by death that is eternal separation from him. This separation is in effect here on earth and produces a life that is not the abundant life Christ promised to his followers. It is a life filled with temporal pleasures, if they are available, that ultimately do not satisfy. Sinners will pay the penalty for their sins.

Nobody can change what God decided and revealed. The only way out from receiving this penalty is through faith in Jesus Christ. To water down this truth is a grave injustice toward those who need God's forgiveness. Why would we do it? No public opinion, no redefinition of sin, and no pressure from the new psychiatrists should dissuade us from proclaiming God's truth. Especially, since we know that no psychiatrist can forgive sins. He can analyze the situation at hand. He can suggest some steps for improvement of the mental condition, but he is powerless to forgive. This is possible only with God, "If we confess our sins, he is faithful and just and will forgive us our sins and purify us from all unrighteousness" (I John 1:9).

Step three. Jesus Christ provides the best solution for our sin problem. The most exciting part of our witness is in offering people the finished work of salvation. Because God loves all people, he is demonstrating his love for all sinners through Jesus Christ and his death on the cross. The amazing thing is that, "While we were yet sinners, Christ died for us" (Romans 5:8). If we had to improve our natural instincts and dispositions, we would be in serious trouble. None would make it to heaven. God knew that very well and was willing to provide a way that would be simple and achievable for all people of the earth. The way is faith in Jesus Christ as our Lord and Savior. Jesus proclaimed it himself, "I am the way and the truth and the life. No one comes to the Father except through me" (John 14:6). This verse is in the very center of much heated discussions coming especially from the postmodern people who deny the truthfulness of these words. Some say Jesus did not make this claim. How do they know it? Do they know more about the teachings of Jesus in the 21st century than the apostle John who listened to him for three years? All these objections are done in the name of pluralism and tolerance, rather than after a serious research into the validity of that statement. It is more convenient for secular people to try to find their own way to heaven than to submit to Christ as their Savior. They prefer a way of no commitment and no accountability. Are we going to give up on asserting that the words of Christ are normative? Absolutely not!

Liberal Christians are claiming that there are many ways to heaven especially those ways described in other world religions. All those millions of people that belong to other faiths cannot be wrong, they say. These discussions boil down to the source of our authority. Christians claim and believe that Jesus Christ is the Son of God (John 1:1, 14), who lived, died on the cross for our sins, rose from the dead and ascended to heaven, and is coming back to judge the living and the dead (I Cor. 15:1-5; II Tim. 4:1). Our witnessing must be always Christocentric. We preach Christ. Paul's instruction to Timothy is fitting here, "Preach the word; be prepared in season and out of season; correct, rebuke and encourage with patience and careful instruction. For the time will come when men will not put up with sound doctrine. Instead, to suit their own desires, they will gather around them a great number of teachers to say what their itching ears want to hear. They will turn their ears away from the truth and turn aside to myths. But you, keep your head in all situations, endure hardship, do the work of an evangelist, discharge all the duties of your ministry: (II Tim. 4:2-5). Paul's prophetic words speak directly to our times. Myths told by mere men are more acceptable in our world than the inspired words of God. Yet, the charge to be an evangelist is for us as well. An evangelist is the proclaimer of the good news. The gospel must be truthfully presented to those who are ignorant of it so that they can believe and accept Jesus Christ as their Savior.

Step four. You must believe in Jesus Christ if you want to be a winner forever. The verb 'to believe' is not always properly understood. To believe some facts about Jesus

Christ is not sufficient. James states clearly, "You believe that there is one God. Good! Even the demons believe that – and shudder" (James 2:19). To know about Christ and not to surrender to him leaves the important question: "How do I save myself?" People have tried it in many ways through good works, self-made religion, improved morality, and increased knowledge. This is what God thinks about human efforts to enter God's kingdom, "All of us have become like one who is unclean, and all our righteous acts are like filthy rags; we all shrivel up like a leaf, and like the wind our sins sweep us away" (Isaiah 64:6). You really do not want to choose this path. You are free before God to make any decision, but you will have to face the consequences that Isaiah spelled out for us.

There is a better response. You have nothing to lose and everything to gain. Think about it for a moment. Believing in Jesus will usher you into God's family. God the Father will accept you without any reservation, "Yet to all who received him, to those who believed in his name, he gave the right to become children of God – children born not of natural descent, nor of human decision or a husband's will, but born of God" (John 1:12-13). This new position is available only because all your sins are forgiven. You experience a brand new beginning, "That if you confess with your mouth, "Jesus is Lord," and believe in your heart that God raised him from the dead, you will be saved. For it is with your heart that you believe and are justified, and it is with your mouth that you confess and are saved" (Romans 10:9-10). God will enter your life through his Spirit to be with you forever, "And do not grieve the Holy Spirit of God, with whom you were sealed for the day of redemption" (Eph. 4:30). Here is the secret of the victorious life: God with us, not just for the very first moment of our belief, but forever.

Do you want to accept Jesus Christ now? You can because Jesus says to you, "Here I am! I stand at the door and knock. If anyone hears my voice and opens the door, I will come in and eat with him, and he with me" (Rev. 3:20). This is the way you will make sure that future victories will be yours, however, they will not be automatic. Christ is a demanding Savior. Listen to his words, "If anyone would come after me, he must deny himself and take up the cross daily and follow me" (Luke 9:23). Christ's disciples are called, as Webber states, "to participate in Christ's victory over evil, to extend Christ's victory in every area of life in which they live and serve, to bring all of life under the reign of Christ."[26]

Some practitioners of evangelism find it helpful to use a baseball diamond to remember the four steps of gospel presentation. I think it is fitting especially for sports evangelism because baseball is such a popular sport and yields itself to a visual aid known to many. The movement from the first base to home plate is the necessary progression for winning.

First base: God created you, loves you, and wants you to be a winner.
Second base: The gravest problem of all people is sin.
Third base: Jesus Christ provides the best solution for our sin problem.
Home plate: You must believe in Jesus Christ if you want to be a winner forever.

This illustration depicts well the process of moving from a self-centered life to the abundant life centered in Christ and committed to Christ. Reaching home plate is not the end of the game in most cases. The game goes on and players must score more runs before the final victory is achieved. We can use this analogy for communicating the truth that is often neglected, namely, that the Christian life demands a great effort all the time till we meet our Savior. One home run follows another one as we grow into mature disciples of Christ. There is no room for relaxing in the race we run and in the fight we fight. Some of you feel tired as you read these lines. But think about it this way. Have you ever seen a winning race car driver take a ten minute break while the race is on? Have you ever seen a football player exit the field when he is given the assignment of catching the ball? And have you ever seen a golfer on the 18th hole deciding it is too hot to hit another ball toward the final green? No, these athletes know the importance of staying the course. Can we do anything less than these athletes? No! Therefore, we need to explain to new believers that finishing the course victoriously is demanding but also rewarding.

Sharing your personal testimony. In the postmodern world the most powerful message centers in our personal experience with Christ. Some people will not accept biblical verses because the Bible is just another book for them. Others will reject theological arguments for the existence of God. Their refusal is based on their hesitation to accept Christian ideas as the absolute norm for relating to God. Do not other religions present similar ideas? Why should they get stuck just with Christian opinions? And finally, there are those who do not want to open themselves up to any religious solutions for their doubts and struggles concerning purpose for life.

This situation changes immediately when we offer to share our personal experience. Everyone tries to make sense out of life that is often complicated, hurtful, and difficult to figure out. The beauty of a life story is in its simplicity and truthfulness. Nobody can argue against it or deny it. The possibility exists that what works for one person can work for another human being as well. The door is usually wide open when we give our testimony because all people like stories, however, we have to make sure we narrate it well.

The apostle Paul is a good example of presenting his story. We have two of his testimonies written in the Book of Acts 22:1-21 and Acts 26:2-23. Both testimonies include three main points. First, Paul described his life before conversion. His passion was to show his devotion to God by persecuting Christians and delivering them to prisons. He seemed to please the High Priest and the whole council of elders by trying to erase the Christian sect from the face of the earth. He traveled to different cities to seek out and punish believers in Christ. Second, Paul explained how he was converted from being a persecutor of Jesus Christ and his followers to becoming Christ's disciple. It happened on the way to Damascus when a blinding light from heaven stopped him in his pursuit of Christians. There he heard the voice of Jesus of Nazareth, received direction from him, and never turned back. His conversion was from doing the evil work, to living for Christ and loving all people. This change was for real and Paul's life turned 180 degrees. Third, Paul demonstrated one time after another that he had a new purpose for his life. He desired to proclaim to pagan people the message of salvation in Christ Jesus. Persecution, suffering, hate, danger on the seas, flogging and stoning could not divert him from living for Christ who saved him. Paul became the greatest missionary of all time as he told his life story throughout the Roman Empire.

Now it is up to us to share our stories about Jesus. Here are some guidelines that will help you in presenting your experiences with God. First, use language that people can understand. Our generation is biblically illiterate. We can no longer presume that people around us read the Bible. They are not familiar with biblical terminology. The turning point happened around the 1950's in America and it is getting worse. Questions like these do not make a lot of sense to unbelievers: "Are you saved?" "Have you been justified by the blood of Christ?" "Have you invited Jesus into your heart?" "Are you enjoying the process of sanctification?" "Have you been redeemed?" "Are you willing to repent of your sins?" We must explain these concepts in simple terms, if we want to make sure we are communicating. The message about our Savior must not change, but since our culture has changed, we must contextualize our proclamation in order to be effective in our proclamation. This is nothing new. Paul had to deliver widely different sermons depending on his audience. Just compare Paul's message to the Jews in Pisidian Antioch (Acts 13:16-41) with the sermon delivered to the Greeks in Athens (Acts 17:22-31). The Jews related to Paul's message based on the Old Testament prophecies, but the Greeks were interested in hearing about gods invented by their poets. The starting points were based on the cultural backgrounds of those listeners, but the final message was clearly the gospel of Jesus Christ.

Second, keep your testimony brief. You never know how much time a person will give you to finish your story. You should be able to narrate it in 3 to 5 minutes. Do not get bogged down by presenting too many details that might not be essential. The purpose of sharing is to point another person to Christ, not to you. If an unbeliever wants to know more and shows enough interest, you can go into a more detailed presentation. It just depends on the situation.

Third, support your testimony with three to four key biblical verses. They will depend on your story. You should choose them well and memorize them so that you can use them even when you do not have your Bible with you. Remember that the Word of God is a two-edged sword (Heb. 4:12). It can penetrate under the artificial mask people wear to protect themselves from outside influences. Then you can trust the Holy Spirit to convict the listener concerning sin and righteousness and judgment (John 16:8).

Fourth, make sure that your life does not contradict your testimony. The first century disciples of Christ were born again people whose transformation was evident to the point of their willingness to die for their Savior and for the Good News they proclaimed. Reid described these Christians in these words, "Their fearlessness in the face of persecution, conviction before skeptics, integrity in a culture of ungodliness, and boldness to proclaim the gospel stands in sharp contrast to the mediocre lives of so many American Christians."[27] Once we profess our faith in Christ, the secular people will watch us to determine whether we are for real. It is a terrible thing if we give them any reason to say that we are hypocrites. No! They should be saying that there is something different about us. Our lives should be sufficiently attractive to them that they would like to meet our Savior and live for him.

Sports background is definitely part of my Christian story, so I will write it as an example for you:

> I was born in Prague in the Czech Republic in 1943 where I lived under the Communist government for 25 years. My father was a Baptist pastor

in Prague and a former professional tennis player. I hesitated to profess my faith in Jesus Christ as my Savior and Lord in spite of the fact that I wanted my sins forgiven. I knew that I would be persecuted for my commitment to Christ and that I would not be able to pursue my plans for my life. When I turned 14, I could no longer say no to God who loved me, "For God so loved the world that he gave his one and only Son, that whoever believes in him shall not perish but have eternal life (John 3:16). Right away I knew that God forgave all my sins and gave me the gift of eternal life. My life overflowed with joy that I could not fully describe.

From that time on my faith was severely tested many times. I was told that it was not quite normal for a young man to believe in God. When I took my entrance examinations at Charles University to major in education, the first question directed at me was, "Do you believe in God?" When I professed my faith in Jesus, one of the professors replied, "We do not need students here who would influence our young people to believe in God. So, your application will be denied." Two years later my ice hockey coach, who was a teacher at the university, tried to convince me there was no God. He gave up after an hour, but before we ended our conversation, he said, "Josef, if you say that you do not believe in God during your next entrance examinations, I can guarantee you that we will allow you to study at this university." He tried to tempt me to deny my Savior, and I considered it for a moment. But then I remembered what Jesus said in Matthew 10:32-33, "Whoever acknowledges me before men, I will also acknowledge him before my Father who is in heaven. But whoever denies me before men, I will also deny him before my Father in heaven. But whoever disowns me before men, I will disown him before my Father in heaven." By God's grace and through the strength he gave me, I stated clearly before five professors that I still believed in God. The door was shut again.

After spending seven years playing professional ice hockey, I applied to study for the ministry at Comenius Theological Seminary in Prague. Knowing that faith in God was essential at a school for pastors, I felt confident that I would be allowed to study there. I received a letter of acceptance from the Seminary, but a governmental official overruled that decision and prevented me from pursuing my goal. He claimed that I would be more beneficial to the Communist society by playing professional ice hockey than if I became a Baptist pastor. A major struggle followed. Should I stay in my home country and disobey the call of God to serve him, or should I escape into the West. The words of the apostle Peter in Acts 5:29 helped me make up my mind, "We must obey God rather than men." So I left my home not knowing whether I would ever see my parents again. It happened during the sixth day of the Russian invasion in August 1968 under the miraculous guidance of God. Russian soldiers searched my car as I was trying to cross the river leaving Prague. Since they stopped me, I offered them a Russian New Testament hoping they would read it and would receive Jesus as their Savior. Czech guards examined my passport at the border and let me cross into Germany. The same week I was awarded a full scholarship at the International Baptist Theological Seminary in Switzerland and my many years of waiting for further education were over. I stayed there three semesters but the theological instruction that I received there was just too liberal for me. I determined to continue my education somewhere else. In 1970 I arrived to

Oklahoma where I played tennis for Oral Roberts University. The tennis team was number four in the nation and I was selected twice All-American in 1971 and 1972. I received my B.A. from ORU in theology in 1972. I continued my education at Southwestern Baptist Theological Seminary in Fort Worth, Texas. I received two degrees from SWBTS, M.Div. (1974) and Ph.D. (1978).

I also served with the Home Mission Board for a year in 1974-75 witnessing to the Czech people living in the metropolitan area of Chicago. After completion of my studies at SWBTS, I worked for Trans World Radio from 1979 to 1980 preaching the Gospel in the Czech language from Monte Carlo, Monaco. Many Czech and Slovak people were saved through this ministry. Upon my return to the States in 1980, I became the pastor of Hulen Street Baptist Church in Fort Worth, Texas where I ministered for 17 years. The church purchased the Fort Worth Racquet Club with 10 tennis courts, a large swimming pool, a soccer field, a softball field, a basketball court, and a volleyball court. Sports evangelism became a very important outreach for HSBC that grew from 70 to 500 members in just three years. I directed evangelistic ministries while being the senior pastor and I encouraged the members of my church to witness to those who came to enjoy our facilities. Many people came to know the Lord because the church opened its doors to everyone who would come to the recreation facilities on the church's property. I also took many church members on mission trips to Europe and South America.

I desired to enlarge my ministry through teaching future pastors and missionaries. Therefore, I accepted the invitation of Dr. Paige Patterson to come to SEBTS in 1997 to teach missions and evangelism. My background in professional ice hockey and tennis in Europe and in the States, combined with my zeal to proclaim the gospel unto all people, prepared me to be a shining example to my students. I continue teaching and motivating my students at SEBTS to be God's ambassadors at home and in the rest of the world. As I look back, I can see God's hand leading me all the way and I can say with Paul, "And we know that in all things God works for the good of those who love him, who have been called according to his purpose (Romans 8:28). Let me ask you a question, "Has anything like this ever happened to you?"

Readiness to witness. Everything you read so far can be wasted unless you get ready to witness. Many Christians know much about evangelism, but for some reason do not get around doing it. Witnessing must be a priority for every disciple of Christ. Paul expressed it in Romans 1:14-15, "I am obligated both to Greeks and non-Greeks, both to the wise and the foolish. That is why I am so eager to preach the gospel also to you who are at Rome." Paul felt he had a debt to pay to all people of his world by presenting the Good News to them. But he went one step further. He confessed his eagerness to preach the gospel.

It is one thing to know about a debt and another thing to pay it. We have the same debt towards people around us and according to God's command, we are to pay it. We can rationalize our inactivity. We can try to place that responsibility on someone else like our pastor or a staff member. Or we can even say that all people will get eventually to heaven, therefore, we do not have to get so uptight about witnessing and paying the debt. These reasons are not biblical. As long as there is one unbeliever in our world, we have to make sure that he hears the gospel. We cannot convert anyone, but we must tell everyone. In order to do it, we should have the same attitude of eagerness as Paul. Eagerness will propel us forward to pay the debt. Just imagine what would happen in our world if more than one billion Christians had the same attitude as Paul. Before long there would not be even one person in this world not knowing about our Savior Jesus Christ. The beginning point is with me and you. Are you ready?

Courage to witness. Eagerness and readiness demand one more ingredient. The effective witness must be courageous. Nothing will get done without courage. Fear can paralyze any Christian no matter how determined he is to spread the gospel. Yet the most pervasive obstacle to evangelism in the lives of committed Christians is fear. There are those who know they should share the gospel and they want to be witnesses, but they are afraid to do so. They give in to the secular environment and become silent. William McRaney interviewed many students and pastors on the subject of evangelism. He concluded that, "fear is the number one-barrier to personal evangelism. Fears are real and imaginary, small and huge, have merit and are unfounded."[28] Fears come at us unexpectedly from every direction, but they do not originate with God. Paul instructed Timothy, "For God did not give us a spirit of timidity, but a spirit of power, of love and of self-discipline. So do not be ashamed to testify about our Lord, or ashamed of me his prisoner. But join with me in suffering for the gospel, by the power of God" (II Tim. 1:7-8). Understanding our fears will help us in dealing with them and subsequently replacing them with courage. Whenever we feel fearful to witness, we are giving in to the Evil One who wants to prevent us from sharing the Good News about Christ. The proper attitude is to acknowledge our fears and try to overcome them. Fay and Hodge list four fears: of rejection, of not knowing enough, of offending a friend or relative, of being ridiculed or persecuted.[29]

First, most Christians would agree that they are afraid of rejection as they witness. Nobody likes to be rejected especially when he presents the gospel. I experienced this rejection over and over again when I tried to share my faith with Communists in Czechoslovakia in the 1960's. Most of them were atheists and let me know that I was behind times and that my faith in God was an illusion. They laughed at me and ridiculed me. Even though I played with some of them on the best professional ice hockey team in Prague, I was never quite accepted by the team members outside of the ice hockey stadium. For me, this was very painful. When I became a Baptist pastor in Fort Worth, Texas in 1980, I did a lot of door-to-door visitation. Texans are friendly people, but occasionally I faced a person that did not want to hear my testimony. Sometime I did not get beyond introducing myself as a local Baptist pastor and the door was shut in my face. When there were too many shut doors, I secretly wished that the next door would not open at all.

We can deal with the fear of rejection by realizing that there will always be people out there who will reject the Christian message. Since they are free human beings, they have the right to do so. This fear comes from a misunderstanding of our role in sharing the gospel. We are merely witnesses about Jesus and we should not take rejection personally, unless we get obnoxious as we present the facts from the Bible. But if we proclaim the Good News lovingly and people are not ready to accept what we offer, then they are rejecting Jesus Christ, not us. We are not responsible for their conversion, but we are to love them no matter how they respond.

Remember the prophets in the Old Testament. They had a message from God and they delivered it under all circumstances, favorable and unfavorable. Sometime the Israelites accepted their message and acted upon it. At other times they did not receive their words and questioned whether the prophecy was from the Lord. Did this unfortunate situation stop the true prophets from communicating with the people of God? Certainly not! They kept on proclaiming, "Thus says the Lord." And we must do the same.

Even a courageous missionary like Paul admitted that he came to Corinth in weakness and fear (I Cor. 2:3). When he wrote to the Ephesians, he asked them, "Pray also for me, that whenever I open my mouth, words may be given me so that I will fearlessly make known the mystery of the gospel" (Eph. 6:19). Paul believed that the Ephesians would pray for him, but he also had a theological reason for fighting fear. In II Cor. 5:10-11 he wrote, "For we must all appear before the judgment seat of Christ, that each one may receive what is due him for the things done while in the body, whether good or bad. Since, then, we know what it is to fear the Lord, we try to persuade men." One day we will all stand before God and the things done out of fear of men rather than by faith in God, will be judged as sin. So why should we do it? There is no reason to be influenced by fear of people around us. The only fear admissible and constructive is the fear of the Lord. Yes, we should be afraid to displease Jesus because of our fears. The fear of the Lord can and will help us overcome the fear of rejection.

Second, young Christians face the fear of not knowing enough of the gospel message. They are afraid they will not be able to answer incriminating questions of the unbelievers. And yet, it is a known fact that new Christians lead more people to Jesus than Christians who have been church members for decades. Their zeal takes over and they eagerly obey their Master in presenting the gospel message that is so dear to them. But then they go through some unpleasant encounters and they start questioning their ability. Should they know more? Yes, but that does not mean they should stop witnessing. Should they study the Bible more? Yes, but it should not prevent them from obeying Christ. The message unto salvation is simple and even the youngest Christian can communicate it. You do not have to have a seminary degree to be an ambassador of Christ. Realize that even the most educated Christian does not have the ability to answer all questions about God. Our God is just too awesome for us to know him completely. God claims in Isaiah 55:8-9, "For my thoughts are not your thoughts, neither are your ways my ways," declares the Lord. "As the heavens are higher than the earth, so are my ways higher than your ways and my thoughts than your thoughts." It is also appropriate to admit that you do not know the answer to a difficult question. But you might suggest that you will research the topic with your pastor and come back with a possible explanation.

Third, is the fear of offending a friend or relative. This fear can build up to such proportions that we would rather leave the witnessing to someone else. Yet we are right there for them. Are we afraid of rejection? Do we know enough not to look ignorant of some aspect of Christianity? But most importantly, do we live such a life before them that would point them to Christ? Do we represent Christ so that he would be attractive to them? These are serious questions that might uncover problems in us and in our families. I am always surprised at how many of my students have relatives who are not Christians. Why aren't they effective in witnessing to them? They usually tell me that it is difficult to witness to people who know them well. This should be a positive rather than a negative issue. Determining to live holy lives at home and anywhere else should easily take care of this concern. But how about close friends and acquaintances that we want to keep or need? There is no greater friend than our Savior. The other people in our lives need to hear about him. We can rest assured that whether our friends still want to associate with us or not after sharing the gospel with them, Jesus is powerful enough to work all things for our good (Romans 8:28).

I struggled with this concern when I played on the professional tennis circuit. When I had the opportunity to witness to some players, I would try to figure out when I should do it. Some players are superstitious and dislike to be approached about things that might derail them from their daily focus. And the truth of the matter is that presenting the claims of Christ involves some confrontation. How long should I wait? Should I ask for a sign to know for sure that the green light was on? Then a liberating idea came to me. If I do not trust Jesus with the outcome of something that he asked me to do, there must be a problem in my relationship with him. I either trust him, or I am a victim of fear that God didn't put in my mind. From that time on I was able most of the time to use those opportunities that God gave me. But a word of caution is in place here. Witnessing must be done graciously and with tact under all circumstances even when the opportunity vanishes away. With people we know well, there should be another time to present Christ.

We can solve problems and open up the way of communication. Just try to imagine the tragedy of not doing everything possible to help your family and friends to find the Lord. The best way to handle this responsibility is to love those dear to you in spite of their rejection of Christ. John assures us, "There is no fear in love. But perfect love drives out fear, because fear has to do with punishment. The one who fears is not made perfect in love" (I John 4:18).

Fourth, I know quite a bit about the fear of being ridiculed or persecuted. Living in a Communist country of Czechoslovakia exposed me to that fear more than I desired. Spreading the gospel was against the law. Communists wanted to make an end to Christianity and they followed a plan to do so. They imprisoned many innocent priests and pastors in order to close local churches down. They just did not know what Jesus said about his church, "And I tell you that you are Peter, and on this rock I will build my church, and the gates of Hades will not overcome it" (Matt. 16:18).

The Devil cannot destroy the church, and the Communists cannot do it either. On the contrary, it is the experience of Christians that ridicule and persecutions make them stronger. They count it a privilege to suffer for their Savior. They also feel his presence and enjoy his provisions under stressful conditions. How much more we should resist fear while living in a free country because persecution happens on a much smaller scale. The early disciples of Christ handled fear of persecution with joy, not fear. "The apostles left the Sanhedrin, rejoicing because they had been counted worthy of suffering disgrace for the Name" (Acts 5:41).

Finally, there is the fear of failure, which is not identical with the fear of rejection. Fay and Hodge do not make this distinction, but I think that a Christian can sense the fear of failure even though he sees people saved. The question in his mind is, "Am I winning enough people to Christ? Shouldn't I reach even more who would become followers of Christ?" This fear is unique to people living in the West. We are conditioned to be successful in whatever we do. In sports we admire stars and superstars because they are winners.

In business we want to be like CEOs who make billions by steering their companies in the right direction. In entertainment we enjoy watching superstars coming from Hollywood whose movies can make millions within days. In such an environment we interpret our evangelistic activity as success or failure depending on our results. The fear of failure is preventing many Christians to witness again especially after not seeing anybody responding to their presentation of the gospel in a while.

A simple biblical explanation should remove the fear of failure from our minds. There is not even one verse in the whole Bible that would demand from Christians to be successful in bringing people to their Savior. Jesus gives a command to all his disciples, “Therefore go and make disciples of all nations, baptizing them in the name of the Father and of the Son and of the Holy Spirit, and teaching them everything I have commanded you. And surely I am with you always, to the very end of the age” (Matt. 28:19-20). Going and making disciples of all people is our responsibility. But we cannot convert anybody. It is the task of the Holy Spirit (John 16:8-11), and we should trust him to bring the God-given results. This attitude will take the fear of failure from our minds and we will be able to enjoy being faithful in what we must do. Remember that we are not asked to be successful, just faithful.

I can imagine someone objecting to this observation and asking, "Didn't the early apostles show a lot of success in winning thousands upon thousands to Christ?" From our perspective we could call it success, however, the results happened because, "All of them were filled with the Holy Spirit and began to speak in other tongues as the Spirit enabled them" (Acts 2:4). These disciples were not trying to be successful. They just wanted to present the facts about their Savior in as many languages as necessary for all those foreigners visiting Jerusalem. While doing that they trusted the Holy Spirit to do the rest. Notice that the number of three thousand saved that day was just a side note. No disciples claimed that Pentecost happened as the result of their activity. It was all of God. We had better practice this approach to evangelism.

We can respond to all fears with the power of God. McRaney defines fear as, "a temporary loss of perspective."[30] Fear detracts us from doing the will of God in face of danger. We must regain our perspective as we join God to accomplish his plan for humanity. Obstacles, imaginary or real, must be removed. There is hope for Christians if they are willing to engage their culture by loving people outside the church walls. Again sports evangelism can be the ideal method for the timid. Playing sports opens up many doors for an informal communication that can eventually lead to a discussion about spiritual things. Above all, people like to know that someone loves them. We are to tell them that God loves them unconditionally and supremely.

Passion to see people saved. Athletes have passion for winning. They are willing to sacrifice a lot in order to accomplish their goals. They get exhausted, hurt, discouraged and defeated, but the best of them will not give up. Why? They are passionate about their sport. What an example for us Christians. Why are we willing to give up on our task of witnessing just because one person treated us harshly? Why would we even think of quitting after someone slammed the door in our face? Possibly it is because of a lack of passion.

Paul did not quit being a witness for Jesus Christ till he died. It was his passion to live for his Savior and to make him known that propelled him on and on. He expressed it in Romans 1:16, "I am not ashamed of the gospel, because it is the power of God for the salvation of everyone who believes: first for the Jew, then for the Gentile." Paul removed fear from his thoughts. He proved it by not being ashamed of the gospel. He was convinced that the gospel was powerful enough to save those who would believe. The same gospel has the same power in our time. But as ambassadors of Christ we need the same passion Paul had. John Knox expressed his passion in a prayer, "Lord, give me Scotland or I die." William Booth, the founder of Salvation Army, told the king of England, "Sir, some men's passion is for fame, but my passion is for souls." There is no doubt in my mind that passionate people are not quitters. God will use them as he used Paul and others throughout the Christian history.

We began this chapter on characteristics of a sports evangelism witness by stressing the need for physical fitness. Not caring for our bodies might become an obstacle to an effective witness among those who are exemplary in that area. Having fit bodies must go along with an informed mind that understands the present day culture of postmodernism. To relate to people presupposes that we know where they are and how they think. We must convince secular people that we as Christians do not just live in the past. Contextualizing the gospel will open up the door for spiritual discussions.

I placed the section on spiritual fitness purposefully after the physical and mental preparation. In our world we need to earn our right to speak to people about God. Once we accomplish it, we can proceed by being spiritually fit. Every aspect of this spiritual preparation is vital so that God can use us as his witnesses. I could have included more material, but I tried to be selective in order to stay within the focus on sports evangelism. Now we will move on to describe the purposes, strategies, methods, and goals of sports evangelism.

CHAPTER FIVE

PURPOSE, STRATEGIES, METHODS, AND GOALS OF SPORTS EVANGELISM

The story of a great basketball player, David Robinson, is an example of sports evangelism among those who are nearly the untouchables of our time. Superstars are being protected by their agents and their teams. So it is extremely difficult to get near to those who, in many cases, need God the most.

When Robinson played for Navy, he became the top college player and was the first pick in the 1987 draft. After joining the Spurs in San Antonio, he made his long-awaited dream come true. Yet all the money and his fame didn't quite satisfy him. Something was missing, but he was not sure what it was. No matter what he achieved, it was not enough.

One day in 1991 a courageous pastor, Greg Ball, told Robinson he would like to talk to him about God. Robinson had some interest in spiritual things and so he agreed. The talk lasted a full five hours because of the many questions Robinson asked. They spoke about reading the Bible, loving God, and honoring God by living for him. Robinson concluded that his priorities were messed up. He thought that he accomplished everything in his own strength. He had houses, cars, and just about all the other things he wanted. Yet he failed to realize it was God who blessed him. He didn't thank God for his blessings. Did he really love God?

Robinson expressed his thoughts like this:

> "You can say all you want to say, but if your actions do not back it up, then it means nothing. I realized that day that God had given me so much, and I had never so much as thanked him. I could see his love for me, what he had done for me, how he had stood by me, and how he had been calling out to me. My heart just broke. So that day I just cried. I said, 'Lord, I am so sorry; I am so sorry. I didn't realize I was being like a spoiled brat. I thank you for everything

you've given to me. I mean you blessed me beyond hope, beyond comprehension. And I just want to give it all right back to you. And from this day forth I just want to learn about you; I want to walk with you; I want to hold your hand; I want to love you like I say I love you.' And man, he turned my life around 180 degrees. And he turned my mentality around 180 degrees. And he gave me a joy and an ability to enjoy what I had that I didn't have before....my whole world just opened up....I can't overstate how important my faith has been to me as an athlete and as a person."[1]

The rest of Robinson's professional career confirmed the truthfulness of his words. He was representing Christ on the basketball court with integrity and he was not shy about speaking about his Savior. He combined his Christian witness with a superb performance on the basketball court. He won a scoring championship in 1994 and the next year he was selected as the MVP of the NBA league. He also represented USA on three consecutive Olympic teams in Seoul, Korea, Barcelona, Spain, and Atlanta, Georgia. Finally, Robinson led the Spurs to win the NBA title. To strengthen his witness as a caring Christian and a devoted disciple of Jesus Christ,

Robinson and his wife donated a $5 million gift to establish the Carver Academy at San Antonio Carver's Center. This was most probably the largest donation by an NBA player.

You don't have to be a superstar athlete to do sports evangelism. If it were so, Christians would not be living up to the command of Christ to go unto all nations. We can reach all people when all Christians get involved. Try to imagine what would happen if 1.2 billion Christians decided to speak up for Jesus and to demonstrate the love of Christ in their world - a bold pastor witnessing to a professional athlete, a coach sharing with a teenager, a spectator pointing the person sitting next to him to God, and a professional athlete using his platform of popularity to announce the Good News. Opportunities to do sports evangelism are everywhere. How should we go about seizing these opportune times to witness about Christ?

We need to have our eyes wide open concerning important facts. According to Huizinga, "Play is older than culture, for culture, however inadequately defined, always presupposes human society."[2] If play is older than culture, than play is a part of culture. Play is a distinct form of activity that fulfills a social function. Huizinga continues, "The fact that play and culture are actually interwoven with one another was neither observed nor expressed, whereas for us the whole point is to show that genuine, pure play is one of the main bases of civilization."[3] The universality of play rests in the fact that it is a voluntary activity. Children and adults are free to play and enjoy playing because they have fun doing it. They step into 'another world' by immersing themselves into it with a devotion known only to the players. Their satisfaction and fulfillment is immediate and, at that moment, nothing else is needed. They follow the rules and enjoy the play as long as it lasts. Yet positive memories remain and result in a desire to repeat the whole process again. Therefore, play continues, but the changes are striking.

The process of developing play into sports began in England in the 19th century. With the increased leisure time, people started organizing games where one town was competing against another town, or one school against another school. Athletes saw the need for stricter rules and recordings of results of the games. Different forms of contest eventually acquired the name 'sports'. Participants were divided into two groups: amateurs and professionals. Amateurs were still involved in the true play-spirit, but for the professionals sports became business and the pure quality of play got lost. Huizinga concluded, "The attempt to assess the play-content in the confusion of modern life is bound to lead us to contradictory conclusions. In the case of sport we have an activity nominally known as play but raised to such a pitch of technical organization and scientific thoroughness that the real play-spirit is threatened with extinction."[4] There is biblical evidence in Zechariah 8:5 that play will not cease even in the New Jerusalem, "The city streets will be filled with boys and girls playing there."

This brief explanation of the development from play to games and to sports underscores the variety of the present sports world. Encountering people at play will open the door for an informal and relaxed communication. But penetrating the highly professional sports arena of world class athletes will demand an organizational skill and even willingness to be rejected before finding the best way. Is sports evangelism the ultimate means for reaching our world with the gospel? No, it is just one of the means available to us even though the possibilities are nearly limitless. In order to build a proper groundwork for doing sports evangelism, we must begin by defining our purpose, strategies, methods, and goals.

THE PURPOSE FOR SPORTS EVANGELISM

The statement of purpose must be the beginning of our thinking. Dayton defines purpose "as an aim or a description of why we are doing what we are doing."[5] The overarching purpose for sports evangelism is to give glory to God through proclaiming the gospel to the ends of the earth while using sports as the common ground. Greg Linville specifies six reasons why sports ministry can reach more people than any other Christian ministry in the world:

1. It reaches the largest cross section of people.
2. It specifically reaches secularized, never-churched, dechurched, and other-churched nonbelievers.
3. It specifically reaches the two missing groups of people in most traditional churches – youth and men.
4. It fulfills church growth principles by empowering and focusing on laity.
5. People are most easily influenced by having fun.
6. Athletic and recreational facilities attract people.[6]

Let us look into these six reasons for sports evangelism separately. First, if Paul lived in the 21st century, he would be attending sports events and witnessing to people around him. He would locate tens of thousands of enthusiasts screaming for their team in a crowded sports stadium. This would be the ideal place to start a conversation about spiritual and eternal values. They might ask Paul to quit talking about Jesus, but he would not stop sharing the Good News. They might force him to leave the stadium, but he would be back again because that place was ideal to connect with people who needed Jesus. A beer company did research on the habits of sports fans in order to know how to advertise their product. They discovered through their research that, "75 percent of all Americans watch sports once a week. In addition, 70 percent discuss, read about, or participate in sports daily, and thirty-five million people identify themselves as being avid sports fans."[7] Most of these people are indifferent when it comes to attending a church. They have more fun participating in sports or attending sports events. In the light of these findings, it is surprising that the experts on church growth neglected for a long time the possibility of doing sports evangelism.

We seem to be stuck with a church growth approach that is not working on a large scale. Hirsch observes, "For the vast majority of churches, church growth techniques have not had any significant or lasting effect in halting their decline. Of the 480,000 or so churches in America, only a very small portion of them can be described as successful seeker-sensitive churches, and most of them have fewer than eighty members. What is more, the church in America is in decline in spite of having church growth theories and techniques predominating our thinking for the last forty years – for all its overt success in a few remarkable cases, it has failed to halt the decline of the church in America and the rest of the Western world."[8] Trying to attract people to switch churches by providing ministries they demand, has not produced overall church growth. It is time to start meeting the secular people on their cultural turf. We have to have a missional mind that will recognize that the leisure culture is the place of our needed presence.

Second, sports evangelism ministry can reach the unchurched people who are not knocking on the doors of church buildings. Many of these people have no desire to enter a worship place where they would feel very uncomfortable. They do not understand our Christian terminology and they do not want to wear 'Sunday clothes'. But the situation changes immediately when we go to their places of 'worship' namely the stadium, the public sports facility, the country club, or just the nature park. We do not look different from them, and hopefully we engage in sports activities that provide the necessary common ground. Through repeated engagements, we have opportunities to let them know who we are. If they enjoy our company, they will most probably accept an invitation to have fellowship in our homes. There we can deepen our friendship and eventually speak with them about our Savior Jesus Christ.

The speed of this progression depends on the unchurched and on our God-given wisdom to proceed. Instead of immediate proclamation, we should do cultivation. Sizemore defines cultivation as "a definite continuing effort to win the confidence and friendship of a person so that a teaching and witnessing relationship may be established. Without this cultivation effort, multitudes of people will never be reached."[9] Jesus is our example here. When he walked through Jericho, he saw Zaccheus in a sycamore tree. The first words Jesus spoke were not about salvation. Jesus simply invited himself into Zaccheus' house where he was received gladly. When the disciples of Jesus saw it, they grumbled because Zaccheus was a sinner, or an unbeliever. Jesus did not care about the public opinion. His purpose was to seek and to save those who were lost. His goal was to touch every sinner that crossed his path. The result was the salvation of Zaccheus whose life was miraculously changed. Cultivation can be brief, or it can last for months, but the possibility of conversion is ever present.

Third, there are two missing groups in many churches – youth and men. It is a known fact that when Christian young people leave their homes for college, many of them lose interest to attend a church. Those who did not become Christians in their youth, think that the church is irrelevant and boring. Men, on the other hand, are willing to let their wives go to church while they stay home trying to rest. But both groups will possibly respond to sports activity. You can sign up youth and men for a baseball league or a basketball tournament as players or coaches. They will want to participate in an activity that promises pleasure and fellowship. And when they make friends with Christians, they might want to be with them even on Sunday.

Fourth, no church can grow without the participation of lay people. Not all Christians will teach, preach, witness, or sing in the choir. But potentially every Christian can get interested in sports ministry. The church needs players, coaches, referees, umpires, trainers, organizers, maintenance workers, reporters, registration officers, counselors, and those who will just talk with visitors. These people will get indirectly involved in evangelism by being present and participating in a ministry that is larger than the local church. Each pastor envisions a total participation of his members in the life of the church. Sports evangelism is a natural avenue for empowering Christians to serve and to discover their God-given gifts.

Fifth, win or lose, athletes have fun. How do I know it? They keep on playing their favorite sports. If they did not enjoy sports, they would not come to the same sports facility over and over again to play the same sport. Christians should build on this observation. We are to rejoice in the Lord always, so our demeanor on the court or on the field should demonstrate a double enjoyment. Nonbelievers should look forward to play sports with pleasant and cheerful athletes who do not cheat, cuss, or threaten the opponent. Here we have a unique situation where we can demonstrate the beauty of the Christian life and the Kingdom of God.

Sixth, the recreational facility of a church either attracts or affects participants negatively. As people come to play on the church's property, they immediately form an opinion about the people of that church. Therefore the softball and the soccer fields have to be maintained according to the standards of the community. Just remember what a pleasant feeling you had when you watched a football game in a brand new football stadium. Teams will spend millions on new stadiums because they attract spectators. The unchurched might come for the first time just because they want to play on an attractive field. Proper programming will encourage them to come again and again. They will experience a Christian fellowship that will point them to Christ.

Before our discussion of strategies for sports evangelism, we must say words of caution about our motivation for this ministry. There are wrong and right motives. Here they are.

Avoiding wrong motives

The world of sports is attractive, even seductive. Athletes travel all over the world and as long as they keep on winning, they assume positions of celebrities. They are welcome in the White House, country clubs, best hotels and restaurants, and the ordinary people like to be seen in their presence. Entering this world can cause a feeling of exhilaration and pride. So the first identifiable wrong motive is the desire to build one's ego rather than to be a humble servant of the Lord. The step from doing ministry to building a career among famous stars is a short one. It can happen without a plan. The characteristics of a witness begin crumbling and his usefulness is gone. Presenting the gospel has to be done on the same level whether the witness shares the Good News with a super star or a homeless person. Both of them need Jesus.

The second wrong motive is the lone ranger approach. If you want all the recognition for doing sports evangelism, you will not like to share the spotlight with anybody else. You might have an agenda that is egoistical and material. If so, you will do more harm than good. You should take seriously the need for growing in Christ yourself before trying to help others. The advice of the apostle Paul is appropriate here, "What after all is Apollos? And what is Paul? Only servants through whom you came to believe – as the Lord has assigned to each his task. I planted the seed, Apollos watered it, but God made it grow. So neither he who plants nor he who waters is anything, but only God, who makes things grow. The man who plants and the man who waters have one purpose; and each will be rewarded according to his own labor" (I Cor. 3:5-8). Christianity is a community religion. We are the body of Christ and we have to approach ministry from the standpoint of team work. Our knowledge of the heavenly reward should compel us to a unified effort that would glorify God.

The third wrong motive is the temptation to adjust and to water down our message. In order to register decisions, we might present a gospel that speaks about cheap grace at the expense of the demands of Christ upon his disciples. We have to make sure that our sports evangelism is always Christ-centered rather than man-centered. There is a fine line between these two approaches. Yes, we are about helping athletes to accept Christ, but we should never advocate easy believism such as, "Just accept Christ and he will give you many victories on the field and much satisfaction off the field."

Christ might do some of that, but we know that Christians are not protected from various trials. Disciples of Christ know that trials will happen, but can also consider those trials and tests with joy (James 1:2-3). This is a completely different approach to life and to competition. We are not left alone with our skills and talents. Win or lose, we go on rejoicing in our Lord. False promises would only misguide the person with whom we are sharing the Good News. They might even say they want to believe in Jesus for selfish reasons and later give up their 'faith' because of the lack of desired results.

There is a better way to approach sports evangelism by making sure we have the right motives and the proper message.

Establishing right motives

The first right motive is the desire to identify with Jesus Christ in his effort to seek and to save what was lost (Luke 19:10). Jesus said these words while he was entering Jericho on the way to Jerusalem. There was no reason to stay around because of time constraints to enter Jerusalem triumphantly to complete the work of salvation on the cross. But there was a lost man in the crowd whose name was Zacchaeus. Jesus immediately changed his plans and looked up to address the man who climbed the sycamore tree. He said, "Zacchaeus, come down immediately. I must stay at your house today" (Luke 19:5). The verb 'must' represented the idea of an absolute necessity.

Our identification with Jesus will sometimes mess up our plans. Instead of pursuing our own goals, we will notice hurting people around us. We will have to enter the culture of sinful men and rub shoulders with them. We will have to go to their homes and have fellowship with them. We will use the means of sports to meet them on a regular basis and prove to them that they are valuable to us. We will separate ourselves from those who resent following the example of Jesus. In fact, we read that even Christ's disciples joined in the grumbling. They did not get it. But we must be willing to identify gladly with Jesus if we want to rejoice in the salvation of unchurched people.

The second positive motive is our desire to obey our Lord Jesus Christ. The command to go and to make disciples of all nations is clear. There is no discipleship without constant obedience. The problem that we face is that obedience of Christ's commands is costly. This is evident in what Jesus said to his disciples before his ascension, "Peace be with you! As the Father has sent me, I am sending you" (John 20:21). Reaching the people of the world will not happen, if we are not ready to take up the cross. Peters explains,

"Whatever else cross-bearing may mean, it certainly implies such voluntary identification with the Lord that he absorbs our love, devotion, time, talent and strength to such a degree that nothing and no one else matters in our life except the Lord. Self-interest, plans, pleasures, position and relations have been denied; self is dethroned and delivered to the Spirit to be crucified. Discipline, limitations and dependence are accepted to follow the Master at every cost and at any expense, even the expense of life."[10] Christ brought the ultimate sacrifice on the cross for our salvation. Now he is asking us to be obedient to him as he was obedient to his Father. There should be no obstacle big enough for us to overcome on the path of radical obedience. The example is before us and the possibilities of Christ's given results are unlimited. Are we going to engage the people of the world in their favorite activities to fulfill the Great Commission? The door is wide open for those who will obey.

The third positive motive is the realization of the urgency to win the world for Christ. Four billion people still do not know our Savior and that number is growing every day. We must discover more effective ways of doing evangelism. Einstein claimed that it is insane to do the same old things, the same old way, and expecting different results. Sports evangelism is a way that fits the post- modern culture, but only the realization of the urgency to win people around us for Christ will propel us in that direction.

Paul records the necessary progression that shows the proper attitude of an evangelist who is convinced of the importance of his task, “I am obligated both to Greeks and non-Greeks, both to the wise and the foolish. That is why I am so eager to preach the gospel also to you who are at Rome. I am not ashamed of the gospel, because it is the power of God for the salvation of everyone who believes: first for the Jew, then for the Gentile” (Romans 1:14-16). The initial recognition in Paul’s mind was the obligation he sensed before God to evangelize all people. He did not exclude anyone. The debt was so enormous that it demanded an immediate action. Therefore, he wrote that he was eager to get on with his task to preach the gospel.

Many Christians are aware of their obligation to spread the Good News. They hear sermons about it. They read about it during their bible studies, but they are not eager to become witnesses. They wish that the staff people would do it since they support them financially so that they would have enough time to be involved in evangelism. The problem then is in the lack of eagerness to share the gospel. It is a known fact that only three to five percent of Christians are intentional witnesses. A possible solution to this problem is in verse 16 where Paul explains the secret of his determination to go to all people and tell them about Christ. If we can truly say with Paul that we are not ashamed of the gospel, because it is the power of God for the salvation of everyone who believes, then we would want to become channels for releasing this power in the rest of our world. If we are eager and not ashamed, sports evangelism can open doors for us in every country of the world. These opportunities are before us and we must make sure that we properly balance sports activities with proclamation. To pursue our purpose, we will define strategies for doing sports evangelism.

STRATEGIES FOR SPORTS EVANGELISM

We live in a fast paced world. Change is all around us. Nobody can keep up with all developments in science, communication, and politics. How can we then plan for the future? We, as Christians, have the advantage of knowing that our God holds the key to all future events. Trusting God then enables us to interpret the future from his perspective and to plan according to our knowledge as revealed in the Bible. As we mentioned in the beginning of this chapter, we have a purpose to reach our world for Christ. No cataclysmic events in our country or in our world will relieve us from this responsibility. We are to move forward planning for the fulfillment of our task, while trusting God to sustain and empower us to accomplish his will for us individually and corporately. Faith in God is an important part of this paradox where tension exists between the awareness of God's sovereignty and man's responsibility. Solomon expressed it in these words, "In his heart a man plans his course, but the Lord determines his steps" (Proverbs 16:9).

The process of planning begins by formulating a strategy. Dayton defines strategy as, "an overall approach, plan, or way of describing how we will go about reaching our goal or solving our problem. Its concern is not with small details."[11] God commissioned Paul to bring the gospel to the Gentiles. So Paul formed at least three strategies. He focused his ministry on large cities like Ephesus, Corinth, Athens, and Rome to reach Gentiles. He started preaching in local synagogues where he met Jews, proselytes, and the curious people who spread the news about his proclamation of Jesus. Finally, he planted a church wherever there were converts to Christianity and then he moved on. God blessed this strategy so much that the church spread from Damascus all the way to Spain through a man who planned, strategized, and was willing to suffer for the cause of winning people for God's kingdom.

Dayton lists three strategies used by Christians to do ministry. First is a "Standard Solution Strategy." The proponents of these strategies presume that because of the past successes, the same strategies can be used again and again in any part of our world. This approach does not take into account the fact that people are not the same everywhere. A distribution of Gospel tracts can be effective in a literate society, but is meaningless in a country where the majority of people cannot read. Second is a "Being-in-the-Way Strategy." This strategy looks down on human planning because it hinders the work of the Holy Spirit. The evangelist simply begins his ministry and then allows God to do the rest. Ministering within this kind of structure provides a way out for the missionary because everything is supposedly the will of God. No wonder that Dayton prefers the third possible strategy which is the "Unique Solution Strategy." He claims that this third "approach believes that we can sketch the outline of a well-thought-out "Solution" to the question of how a given people could be effectively evangelized. We are not ruling out visions, dreams, or sudden convictions.

Planning uses whatever resources are authentically given to us by the Spirit of God. The idea that the Holy Spirit does not use human preparation in doing the work of the kingdom is inadequate to Scripture and experience."[12] We will adopt the Unique Solution approach because it avoids extremes presented in the two previous strategies. We will depend on the guidance of the Holy Spirit as we seek to be wise in putting in place strategies that would enhance our involvement in sports evangelism. This approach is especially crucial for a world wide ministry that can touch all cultures and all people groups in the world. But a similar challenge is before us even if we minister in just one country such as the United States of America. Plurality of cultures is a fact of life and each people group is unique. Considering the variety of ethnic groups in America gives us an idea how much more we need to pay attention to cultures in foreign countries. The only thing we can depend upon is the ingrained love for play and sports in the human soul. Beyond that we must be open to new strategies, implement them, and if necessary, change them on the spot.

Changing the Unique Solution strategy might not be an easy task because we usually do not want to admit that we made a mistake. Here comes into play our total dependence on the Holy Spirit. Paul wanted to go to Bithynia, but the Spirit of Jesus prevented him to go there. He could have insisted on his original plan. He could have said, "I just misunderstood what God is trying to tell me." But Paul was sensitive to the guidance of the Spirit of God and simply accepted the new direction. He passed by Mysia and ended up in Troas. Being in the place where God wanted him resulted in a new vision, "After Paul had seen the vision, we got ready at once to leave for Macedonia, concluding that God had call us to preach the gospel to them" (Acts 16:10). After some traveling, Paul and his group arrived in Philippi, the leading city of that district of Macedonia. Paul had to adjust his usual strategy to preach in a local synagogue because there was not even one synagogue in Philippi. So he went outside the city gate to the river where he found a place of prayer. He then made another adjustment and started to speak to the women who assembled there. A fertile ministry followed and Paul was able to plant a church on the European soil. Imagine what would have happened if Paul insisted on his original plan. Would he ever venture into Europe? We will never know. But we know that even the best strategy should be scrutinized from God's perspective from time to time.

There are three levels of strategy according to Dayton - a grand strategy, an intermediate strategy, and a short-range strategy.[13] Following this structure, we should begin by accepting the responsibility to provide for the evangelization of all sports minded people in every country of the world. Then we should plan to visit places where people play sports or watch sports events, or we should organize sports competitions in local churches. These activities would build bridges to secular people on a regular basis with the view of establishing meaningful relationships. Finally, we should encourage sports evangelists to start inviting people to specific events where they would be exposed to believers who would be demonstrating the Christian way of life to them.

This strategy can be implemented in every nation, but it is not the Standard Solution Strategy. A careful analysis must precede the beginning of sports evangelism based on the popular sports in a given country. You would not get anywhere by sending an ice hockey team to Brazil. When I preached in revival meetings in Belo Horizonte, Brazil, I wanted to share an experience from playing ice hockey in the Czech Republic. As soon as I mentioned 'ice hockey' my interpreter whispered into my ear, "What is ice hockey"? I answered, "It is like playing soccer, but the field is covered with ice and the players have to have skates on their feet in order to move fast and get to the puck which is something like a round flat thing made of hard rubber." The interpreter thought about it for a moment and then he told the audience that I played soccer on ice professionally. I have never seen more confused faces in the audience than at that time. My illustration was very short and rather ineffective.

Or there would be no advantage in sending a football team to the people of Kenya.. No matter how many committed Christians there would be on the team, they would not convince the local people to put on shirts, long pants, helmets and all those pads. They would think it to be crazy and illogical. But they would be open to playing soccer barefooted and barely clad if the team supplied a nice round soccer ball.

Due to the influence of TV programs, many people are interested in learning to play baseball. It is fairly inexpensive to bring bats and balls. Americans can teach baseball in parks and on soccer fields. Since we are good at it, we can do a good job without facing a stiff competition in many countries. The audience will gather and a time of instruction will follow. Building a common ground will enable the teachers to do teaching on the field in a given sport but also sharing their faith at the conclusion of a clinic.

This strategy works at home and abroad. There is no distinction in playing sports in America, Asia, or Europe. The only prerequisite for playing abroad is the presence of an interpreter who can explain what is going on. In fact, this is increasingly the need even in America when we want to minister to immigrants who have not learned to speak

English. We can practice at home what we are supposed to do in the rest of our world.

Sports evangelism can become one of the most efficient outreach ministries in the United States of America where about 70% people are unchurched and 80% of churches are plateaued or declining. Malphurs explains, "The S-curve depicts how virtually everything in life begins, grows, plateaus, and then ultimately dies....As it relates to the church, the S-curve represents essentially its life-cycle pattern. Like people, churches have a life cycle. In general, a church is born, and over time it grows. Eventually it reaches a plateau, and if nothing is done to move it off that plateau, it begins to decline. If nothing interrupts the decline, it dies."[14] We have already mentioned that we live in a time when changes happen in a faster way than any time before. The S-curve is shrinking and the church, especially in North America, must pay attention to this phenomenon. Can we circumvent this impending danger of dying churches? Malphurs recommends two solutions, "First, gifted leaders of churches and denominations must start new S-curves. They need to launch out in new directions. Second, they need a strategic planning process that helps them start new sigmoid curves. They need to know how to think and act in the twenty-first century."[15] There is nothing easy about starting a new curve in the growth of a church. There is no prescribed formula that would fit all plateaued churches. Pastors and church leaders need to interpret the church situation from the perspective of their own community and decide on the next step of faith. God honors courageous Christians who are not satisfied with the present situation. Joshua did not want to remain idle outside the Promised Land. God had better plans for his chosen nation and so he communicated with Joshua, "Be strong and courageous, for you shall give this people possession of the land which I swore to their fathers to give them" (Joshua 1:6). Interestingly enough God repeated the same message two more times (verse 7 and 9) to make sure that Joshua would not shrink back. In the same way, we must listen to God and move forward keeping the church on target serving God and reaching people for God's kingdom. The second curve is a good possibility for any church that will step out in faith and reaffirm the call of God to go and make disciples. The unique opportunity for the churches in the twenty first century to move in a new direction is sports evangelism. It is not the only way, but it is one that revitalizes a declining church because of new emphasis on evangelism that fits our postmodern culture.

Whether we are involved in planting churches, revitalizing local congregations, or just trying to proclaim the gospel to unchurched people and making disciples of Jesus Christ, the strategy for sports evangelism will prove effective. This promise, however, depends on Christians relying on the power of the Holy Spirit to make it work. As you already noticed, this strategy is not a fossilized program but a living process developed for each new situation and each new group. Adults, young people, and even children can participate under a skilful leadership that provides a unique solution to use sports in evangelism.

Since I am familiar with the situation in the Czech Republic, I will use that nation as an example of formulating a strategy for doing sports evangelism there. The Czech people boast of a truly secular society where 80% of them claim to be atheists. Conversations with these people go nowhere by starting talking about faith in God. They immediately state that there is no God. Why should they speak about someone who does not exist? They would prefer to learn more about the United States and about the possibility to go there and earn more money.

I tried to make a High School student think about the possibility that God does exist. He answered, "If you show me your God, I will believe in him, but if you are not able to do that, you are wasting your time." I was not going to give up that easily and so I continued, "Do you believe in something that you cannot see like the air that you breathe in and out"? "Yes, I do, but I know what it is." "Well, I know who God is," I said, "because I see the beautiful world that he created and keeps in order." To this the young man responded, "You cannot prove it, but I know that our world just evolved starting with the Big Bang." I knew that this was coming. Children in grammar schools are taught that evolution is a scientific fact. They hear it so many times that they assume there is no other explanation.

This was a turning point in our conversation. I informed him that evolution is merely a theory and that there is no proof of macro evolution. I continued, "All the paintings you saw as you were growing up were just that, only the imagination of an artist who was hired by secularists to paint them to try to convince you that we evolved from apes." "I was not quite sure about those pictures, but they still make more sense to me than believing in a Creator," he retorted. By this time I detected a possible doubt in his convictions, so I pressed on, "Would you like to know about a purpose that would be bigger than just your existence here on earth"? "Oh, I think I determined a purpose for my life. I want to make a lot of money, marry a good looking young woman, and have some kids that I would enjoy." I challenged him, "What will you do if some of these things do not happen"? "Well, I will keep on trying. I am a strong person." All the while this young man thought he had everything figured out. But there was one more question I needed to ask, "Do you believe there is a heaven"? "I am not sure about this pie in the sky talk. I think when I die, it will be simply over." I could not help but to affirm my belief, "I know that I will go to heaven because I believe in Jesus Christ who came to this earth, died for my sins, rose from the dead, and now lives in heaven where he actually prepared a place for me. Jesus Christ is God himself and he can give you an eternal life as well. Would you like to know how"? Honza, that was his name, thought about my question for a while and then he stated, "I can see that you have hope that I don't have, but I am not sure about all of it. This talk is so new to me. Maybe we can get together later and continue our conversation."

I spoke with many young people that had a similar doubtful attitude. I saw some of them only once or twice and then I had to leave the results up to the Holy Spirit. This whole situation would be different if I contacted Honza on a tennis court or on a soccer field. If he enjoyed playing with me, he would be back because he would want to play again. This would provide for a common ground that did not exist in my brief encounters with students in High Schools. Secular people need to hear from us often while observing a real demonstration of the beauty of the Christian life through repeated encounters. I know this plan works because I saw sports minded secular people saved by implementing this strategy.

There is one more issue we have to consider. Strategy must be defined as a process. A plan that worked five years ago might become obsolete. Therefore, there is always a need for an ongoing assessment of a plan that is before us. This can be done through strategic planning that keeps us on track and that makes a difference between a successful ministry and a ministry that has plateaued. Malphurs defines "strategic planning as the envisioning process that a point leader uses with a team of leaders on a regular basis to think and to act so as to design and redesign a specific ministry model that accomplishes the Great Commission in their unique ministry context."[16] Those who are part of this process must be visionaries. They must look beyond the present and try to see a different and better future. They ask, "What is the next model that will fit our church and our community?" "How will we go about making that model work for the glory of our God?" "Is this plan uniquely suited for our church?"

The pastor of a local church should lead in this effort and make sure that the implementation moves in the right direction. But he should also select a leadership team that would provide for a variety of ideas and a multitude of talents. Moses got overworked while trying to judge the people of Israel in the wilderness. He had enough sense to discuss his situation with Jethro, his father-in-law, who advised him to get some help, "But select capable men from all the people-men who fear God, trustworthy men who hate dishonest gain-and appoint them as officials over thousands, hundreds, fifties and tens. Have them serve as judges for the people at all times, but have them bring every difficult case to you; the simple cases they can decide themselves" (Exodus 18:21-22). Paul had no problems formulating his strategy in many cities and countries, but he also saw the need for a team to implement those plans with him. More people thinking and searching the Scriptures in the context of their church, will hopefully come up with a plan that fits their congregation and their community. But even more importantly, the members of the church will be more inclined to accept the model and to put it into action.

Receiving a plan, a model, or suggestions from an associational office or the convention does not guarantee implementation. In fact, many of these well intentioned plans end up in a file, or after several disappointments with similar programs, they will be immediately rejected as something that 'will not work here'. Similar results happen when a pastor attends a conference on church growth, brings new ideas, tries to sell them to his congregation and finds out that the members of his church are not willing to implement them. Strategic planning done by a team selected from the church has a better chance to produce active participation. Description of a plan will not automatically result in action.

METHODS FOR SPORTS EVANGELISM

Defining our methodology is the next step that we must take in order to prepare the way for an orderly way of realizing our strategy. The right methods will put us on a path where we can travel purposefully toward the fulfilling of the goal of our ministry. Dayton states that, "a method is a regular or orderly way of doing something. It is a standardized procedure for producing a given result. Experience or research tells us a method or procedure produces the results we seek. Methods discipline our action and our thought by providing a pre-thought pattern for what we do and how we approach the task."[17] We are embarking on a relatively new approach to doing evangelism and so our methods might not be readily accepted. This fact should not distract us from developing a regular way of using sports for evangelizing the unchurched. If some Christians come at us with the often repeated phrase 'we have never done it this way', we will have to rely more on the guidance of the Holy Spirit than on the preconceived ideas of Christians who value tradition at the expense of seeing multitudes saved.

Motives for evangelism can be wrong and so can our methods. We must proceed carefully, especially since we are treading on fairly new ground. The seductiveness of sports must not deter us from living holy lives in an unholy atmosphere. Imitating the ways of Jesus will provide for proper methodology. We are not at a loss for sufficient information on this subject. The gospels provide plenty of information that reveals the method of Jesus. Coleman stated simply, "Men were his method."[18] Christ had an unassuming method which produced magnificent results throughout twenty centuries. He was able to move from his vision of offering salvation to all people to a practical pattern of making disciples who would continue in proclaiming and living the gospel.

The eightfold method was thoroughly biblical and applicable in all situations and cultures with just one exception. Jesus equipped twelve apostles who were men. Before Jesus left this earth going to his Father in heaven, he spoke these words to men and women who were his disciples, "But you will receive power when the Holy Spirit comes on you; and you will be my witnesses in Jerusalem, and in all Judea and Samaria, and to the ends of the earth" (Acts 1:8). All Christians will be Christ's witnesses; therefore, we must include women in our method to produce mature believers who will know how to use sports evangelism to make Jesus known in all nations. This comment is especially important for cultures where women compete in sports independently from men. Sports like soccer and ice hockey were the domain of men, but now women have their own leagues. They even compete in the Olympic Games in these sports. I am sure that more of these changes will be happening in the near future. Why not then have women penetrating these areas that are reserved for them? Here are Coleman's eight principles describing the method of Jesus.

Selection

From the very beginning we notice something very unusual. Jesus did not follow our preconceived ideas of success. Who would in his right mind select uneducated, ordinary, unimpressive men to accept a world wide assignment? Luke confirms that "they were unschooled, ordinary men" (Acts 4:13). And who would start with just twelve of those men? These are two criteria we would handle quite differently. We demand education and we like big numbers. When a church has a membership of 35 people we think there is something wrong with the pastor and the church itself. We do not evaluate a church at first according to its maturity, worship, ministry, outreach, fellowship, and the ability to plant a church in another country. And yet we would agree that a leader can teach and equip a smaller group better than a large crowd that participates in a three day conference.

The example of Jesus is clear. In the middle of his second year of public ministry, Jesus "called his disciples to him and chose twelve of them, whom he also designated apostles" (Acts 6:13). He could have selected many more to teach and equip because the crowds were always curious about his ministry, but he understood well that effective instruction happened in a smaller group of students.

The beginning of sports ministry does not demand a crowd. We should select those men and women who have passion for Christ and who relate well to sports minded people. Teaching a smaller group should be an easier task. They in turn will be able to select others who will continue the same ministry. The foundation of sports ministry is all important and has to be done with caution. If the ministry crumbles at its beginning due to a lack of commitment and understanding among the workers, the continuation and preservation of that ministry will be in jeopardy. On the other hand, if we are willing to invest our lives into a few selected

Christians who have a vision of reaching the world through sports evangelism, they will carry on what we started.

Association

Jesus changed the educational method from the formal, classroom teaching of the scribes to the informal education as his disciples observed his actions and listened to his words while he was performing his ministry. We would call this education on-the-job-training. Those twelve apostles had the privilege of associating with Jesus on daily basis as they followed him wherever he went. They did not take notes. They simply observed the life of Christ that he supported by his actions. There was no hypocrisy and no adjustments under pressure. What they saw in Jesus was true under all circumstances. Words merely supported his true character. In many cases Jesus did not have to explain his actions because they were not in conflict with what he taught. Coleman describes the result of this principle, "Knowledge was gained by association before it was understood by explanation....One living sermon is worth a hundred explanations."[19] This kind of association was so important to Jesus that his presence with them was more and more intimate as his life here on earth was coming to an abrupt end. Jesus made sure that even after his resurrection this association would not be interrupted. He told them, "And surely I am with you always, to the very end of the age" (Matthew 28:20). There is a great need to recover this approach in developing disciples. In our fast paced world we do not take time for daily encounters. We have a difficult time to get together just once a week on Sundays because we run busily in many directions. No wonder that we are failing in producing disciples that can minister on their own.

Let us suppose that a pastor of a local church is ready to start a sports evangelism ministry. He presents the challenge from the pulpit and about seven people show interest in joining him to reach out to the secular people in their community. The normal procedure would be to have a one day seminar on sports evangelism, give them an assignment and turn them loose. This is a clear cut method for a failed attempt at a new ministry. If the pastor is serious about this new development, he must do the selecting rather than to have people volunteer. Then he must associate with those selected people through a personal example and by asking them for help during sports evangelistic events. He will observe them and they in turn can ask questions that will clarify some things they are not capable of figuring out on their own. As they improve their ability to perform the ministry alongside the pastor, he can ask them to take the leadership position while he is ready to help. There is no substitute for associating with those who want to spread the gospel in an effective way. Jesus was there for his disciples and so we must follow his example closely.

Consecration

The third principle is about the irrevocable devotion to Jesus. Obedience was an integral part of following Christ. Nobody could follow him in an idle manner. They either accepted the conditions of discipleship or they could leave. Jesus presented this call to his disciples in these words, "If anyone would come after me, he must deny himself and take up his cross and follow me" (Matthew 16:24). Denying ourselves and taking up the cross that signified a willingness to die for the cause of Christ seemed to be too radical for some would be followers. John tells us that "many of his disciples turned back and no longer followed him" (John 6:66). Jesus did not go after deserters. He knew he could not rely on them. He wanted only those who were consecrated unto him, who counted the cost and stayed. That is why he asked even his twelve apostles whether they wanted to leave. That option was before them. However, Peter vowed for himself and for the rest of the apostles, "Lord, to whom shall we go? You have the words of eternal life. We believe and know that you are the Holy One of God" (John 6:68-69).

By now they sensed they were following the Messiah who was worthy of their worship and trust. Did they understand everything that was going on? Certainly not! But Jesus was willing to teach them and would not allow any compromise. All he wanted from them at this point was a commitment to him as a person. We can see it in his demand, "Take my yoke upon you and learn from me, for I am gentle and humble in heart, and you will find rest for your souls. For my yoke is easy and my burden is light" (Matthew 11:29-30).

Consecration unto Christ is an overlooked demand in the present day discipleship. Complacency and mediocrity is tolerated for the sake of numbers, statistics, and money. Unregenerate membership is on the rise and consecration unto Christ is very low. It begins with the way we accept people into our churches and it continues in lowering standards of a true Christian life. The final result is a church as a whole that is not that much more different from the world. It is absolutely necessary that we change this situation if we want to do sports evangelism. We will not be able to teach sports and to compete in sports on the same level as it is done in the world. We do not have those high performing athletes who mesmerize millions of fans. We do not have stadiums where thousands upon thousands can gather to watch a football game or a car race. We do not have highly qualified coaches and general managers that run professional teams.

What can we offer? We have to present Christ who changed our lives and who gave us a purpose for living that cannot be found anywhere else. But if we are not demonstrating the new of life in Christ, we had better stay in our sanctuaries and hope we can somehow survive the onslaught of secularism. If we do that, and some churches have already chosen that approach, then we are not living up to the words of Paul who wrote, "As it is written, 'For your sake we face death all day long; we are considered as sheep to be slaughtered.' No, in all these things we are more than conquerors through him who loved us" (Romans 8:36-37). The word 'conquer' is definitely a part of sports vocabulary. It expresses the ultimate goal of any athlete to destroy his opponent and to gain the winner's prize at that particular moment. For a Christian, to conquer means here on earth as well, but the prize for conquering will be presented when we already enjoy the eternal life in God's presence. This reward, however, depends on our deeds while we follow Christ during our earthly life. Doing sports evangelism will produce deeds that God will reward. Consecration to Christ is a prerequisite for such a ministry. Demanding consecration is biblical and of utmost importance in our secular world.

Impartation

Leaders must be willing to impart themselves in the lives of their students and coworkers. Jesus gave his disciples everything they needed. He gave them peace, joy, keys to his kingdom, and his glory. The final gift of Jesus before leaving this earth was his Spirit, "And with that he breathed on them and said, 'Receive the Holy Spirit'" (John 20:22). Now that they had his Spirit living in them, they were ready to have the same passion that consumed all of his life, namely, to seek and to save those who were lost.

We do not need to repeat what Jesus did for his apostles. The gift of the Holy Spirit is given to every believer in Jesus Christ immediately at the time of faith in him. But we need to teach those who want to be involved in sports evangelism to depend on the Holy Spirit (Rom. 8:9). Surprisingly the teaching about the Holy Spirit is not prominent in preaching and teaching of many pastors. They preach about God the Father and about Jesus Christ, but fail to give the same attention to the Holy Spirit. Yet, he is the One who converts people. He performs a supernatural act of conversion as we share the gospel with unbelievers. I believe that those interested in sports evangelism have to know what the Holy Spirit desires to do through them. Only then they will obey the command to be continuously filled with the

Spirit of Christ (Eph. 5:18). If that is true, they will be able to trust the Spirit with the ministry that they want to do in the enemy's territory. Coleman claims, "Jesus was God in revelation; but the Spirit was God in operation. He was the Agent of God actually effecting through men the eternal plan of salvation."[20] The presence of the Holy Spirit in evangelistic efforts makes them a divine project. It is not just our work but God's. We cannot fail while cooperating with the Holy Spirit. When we die to ourselves we make room for God to bring eternal results.

Demonstration

The fifth principle is of great value in the 21st century. We are bombarded each day with information about people in just about every corner of our world. There are no more secrets. Once something becomes news, the world has an access to it. The World Wide Web has the capability to disseminate information within seconds whether it is good or bad. Usually the bad news is more attractive because the good news is hard to come by. Communication technology can be a valuable means for proclamation of the Good News. But when Christians get caught living immoral and hypocritical lives, the news hurts the reputation of the church and the criticism becomes vicious.

Jesus demonstrated a holy life before his apostles. The testimony about him claimed that he lived a sinless life (I Peter 2:22). He was the only one who could say without any hesitation, "I have set you an example that you should do as I have done for you" (John 13:15). The apostles learned from Jesus as they observed his daily actions. He did not have to produce a manual on evangelism. He practiced evangelism in such a way that his apostles desired to imitate his actions. His demonstration was so powerful and impressive that his followers could duplicate it without hesitation.

A pastor in a local church might not be equipped to demonstrate the ministry of sports evangelism, but he can pray about it and take necessary steps to gain insights into sports ministry on his own. If he has merely a nebulous idea about reaching people through sports, there is also a possibility that a lay person has some experience in sports and would like to start sports evangelism. Seeking God in prayer and proceeding slowly is the approach to a new ministry.

Delegation

The church is the Body of Christ (Col. 1:24). Every Christian should take part in different functions of the church. Why is it that some pastors and leaders do not trust other Christians to minister within the church? Is it because they think nobody else can do the job as they do? Or is it because they lack the ability to delegate ministries to qualified workers? No matter what the answers, the fact is that delegation will involve Christians in ministries that the Holy Spirit can bless. Jesus made it clear at the beginning of his association with his apostles that following him would demand engaging in work, "Come, follow me," Jesus said, "and I will make you fishers of men" (Matt. 4:19). The timing of delegating outreach ministries to his apostles is significant. It seems that at the beginning, for about a year, the apostles did not get involved in evangelistic work. Jesus waited till he led them for the third time through Galilee. Then he sent them out into the surrounding areas. They were selected long before they were sent as is seen in Matthew 10:5-8, "These twelve Jesus sent out with the following instructions; 'Do not go among the Gentiles or enter any town of the Samaritans. Go rather to the lost sheep of Israel. As you go, preach this message: 'The kingdom of heaven is near.' Heal the sick, raise the dead, cleanse those who have leprosy, drive out demons. Freely you have received, freely give." Notice the clarity of instruction. Jesus developed a strategy before he asked them to reach out. They were to go first to the Israelites. Those were the people of similar cultural background. They were the first on the apostles' agenda because they would understand the news of the coming Messiah. But the proclamation of the kingdom had to be accompanied by miracles performed in the power of Jesus who sent them.

A few months later Jesus delegated the same task to seventy two other disciples and sent them two by two to enter every town where he would be preaching and teaching. But this time the strategy changed. There was no limitation put on these disciples. They were to go everywhere as long as the people of those towns welcomed them, "Go! I am sending you out like lambs among wolves" (Luke 10:3). Delegation must be done in a thoughtful way. Details must be worked out and if necessary the strategy must change. If danger lurks around the corner, we should warn our ministers and let them decide whether they want to do risky business for the building of God's kingdom here on earth.

The leader who entrusts ministry of evangelism to others must lead by his example. Jesus did exactly that. "After Jesus had finished instructing his twelve disciples, he went on from there to teach and preach in towns of Galilee" (Matthew 11:1). People will follow a pastor who shows passion for those things he demands from them. Sports evangelism will not get done in a church where there is nobody to take the lead. Someone has to have a position of authority and trust to train the people and to challenge them by giving them a specific assignment. There are enough people in our churches who will respond positively.

I was struggling in getting more of my people involved in evangelism. I knew that doing outreach just on my own would not produce sufficient results and that it would only solidify the notion that lay people do not have to witness about Jesus. They pay the pastor and so he has all the time to do ministries alone, doesn't he? No, he does not. Especially in the area of witnessing, the command of Christ is clear. Every gospel records the words of the resurrected Christ to go into the world and to make him known. Therefore, a pastor has to find a way how to delegate this important ministry. Since I know that Christ's method is men, I devised a plan. I told the members of my church that I would like to train them to be witnesses about Jesus Christ. I preached on the importance of obeying Christ's commands and on the tremendous satisfaction his witnesses experience when they step out in faith doing evangelism. Then I set a date on Saturday morning from 9:00 to 12:00 followed by a delicious lunch at the church (eating together works real well to bring Baptists to church). To my surprise two thirds of the church showed up. I tried to make the training as interesting as possible and at 11:30 I made my concluding remarks. Even though our ladies were already cooking lunch, I had 30 minutes to do something else.

At this point I tried something I was not sure about but I did it anyway. I asked everyone present to join me to go into the streets around the church to put into practice what we just studied. I said, "Thank you for studying with me how to evangelize our community. You participated really well, but now is the time to go and share the gospel with others. I am going to do it for the next 30 minutes and I would like for you to join me. However, I did not tell you ahead of time that this is what I wanted to do. So if you want to go, I will be glad to see you in the bus and take you to our neighborhood. But I am not going to force you to go. You can stay here and wait till we get back exactly at 12:00. I am really looking forward to our fellowship as we eat together." After I said this I moved out of the sanctuary and on to the bus. I thought to myself, "I hope somebody will go with me. It would be rather unpleasant to be driving the bus alone." Before I opened the door of the bus, people were going out of the church and in a few minutes all students joined me to speak for Jesus in our neighborhood.

Giving specific assignments to people who love Jesus works. If we do not delegate, some Christians will not ever do evangelism. They will leave it up to professionals. There is a better way if we are serious about proclaiming the gospel unto the ends of the earth. The way can be summarized in one word – delegation. Evangelism is not one of many options for the disciples of Christ. It is the highest calling from Christ himself to us. Since sports evangelism demands large numbers of helpers to organize and supervise sports activities, delegation will be at the very center of that ministry.

Supervision

Association, consecration, impartation, demonstration, and delegation must be supported by a constant supervision. Jesus practiced it by moving from instruction to assignment and on to checking up on his apostles. When the twelve returned from their mission among the Israelites, they reported to Jesus about their actions and teaching. People around them were disrupting this session so Jesus asked them, "Come with me by yourselves to a quiet place and get some rest" (Mark 6:31). Jesus was willing to spend this important time just with his apostles. Although he knew what was happening, he wanted to assure them that he was vitally interested in everything they wanted to share with him. His comments provided true interpretation of what was happening on the field. He determined whether their ministry was done according to his expectations. When the group of seventy two came back, they claimed that even the demons submitted to them because they cast them out in Jesus' name. The answer Jesus gave them kept things in proper perspective, "I saw Satan fall like lightning from heaven. I have given you authority to trample on snakes and scorpions and to overcome all the power of the enemy. However, do not rejoice that the spirits submit to you, but rejoice that your names are written in heaven" (Luke 10:18-20). Jesus rejoiced in the good report, but he immediately directed them to think about the most important thing and not to get their egos inflated. Jesus envisioned the conquest of the whole world, but he did not demand more than what they could do. He had the master plan and was willing to trust the following generations to continue in evangelistic efforts.

Our difficulty is in not knowing fully what we should expect. Should we plan for one hundred conversions in a week long sports clinic? Or should we trust God with three thousand conversions as it happened in Jerusalem at Pentecost? It would be absurd to expect more conversions than the number of participants. But we can approach this matter from the perspective of preparation. Did we do all we could to get as many participants to the clinic as possible? Did we delegate responsibilities properly? Did we supervise closely enough the whole operation? Did we pray enough?

Did we really expect God to do something miraculous? We really cannot answer these questions to our full satisfaction. Coleman advises, "We fail, not because we do not try to do something, but because we let our little efforts become an excuse for not doing more. The result is that we lose by default the advantage of years of hard work and sacrifice."[21] Realistic supervision can encourage witnesses of Christ to higher achievements and perseverance in doing evangelism.

Reproduction

We come to the final principle of the method of Christ. It is mentioned strategically at the very end. Every part of this method is important, yet without reproduction of disciples, everything will eventually fail. We would be just spinning wheels, if we were producing disciples who do not evangelize and who do not take seriously the command of Christ. In fact we could question the genuineness of those disciples that would give up their commitment at the point of reproduction. The early disciples counted the cost and moved on boldly reproducing themselves throughout their world. They obeyed their Master who demanded multiplication of disciples, "You did not choose me, but I chose you and appointed you to go and bear fruit – fruit that will last. Then the Father will give you whatever you ask in my name" (John 15:16).

Notice that Christ attached a great promise to those who will bear fruit. As if he was saying, "First do what I tell you to do, and then you can receive whatever you ask from me." Quite often we think we need to be fervent in prayer before we can expect God's answers. This is true when we combine prayers with actions. We must not separate these two disciplines.

Bearing fruit is closely connected in the mind of Christ with making disciples. The power for bearing fruit is available through the presence of the Holy Spirit in us. We must recover this method in its entirety even if we have to focus on small groups just as Christ did. The question before us is, "Are new converts maturing into leaders that can make disciples and perpetuate the cycle of new disciples?" It is not enough in the ministry of evangelism to bring people to Christ and to see them committing their lives to him. We must continue in the Master Plan of Christ by producing those who can reproduce themselves in God's kingdom.

I claim that sports evangelism can facilitate this method of evangelizing better than any other approach. It opens up the door for relationships with those who are not interested in Christ, but who enjoy sports. Once a relationship is established, there is a possibility that those people will listen to us. By God's grace and through the work of the Holy Spirit we will see some of these secular people come to know

Jesus as their Savior. Because we enjoy playing sports with these new Christians, we have a unique opportunity to disciple them in church and in the stadium. More encounters provide for more possibilities to apply the method that Christ used. If we recover these principles, we will not need new programs and slogans. We will be producing men and women that will make disciples who in turn will continue reaching the world.

Since a method is a regular and orderly way of doing something, Christians have to decide what the orderly way is for them. This decision depends on the cultural context of their living environment and on the possibilities before them. There are countries where Christians are free to attempt just about anything within a free society. There are other Christians whose freedom is limited by a local government. They are forced to stay in their sanctuaries. And there are some Christians who are oppressed and persecuted for their faith. They hope to survive in an underground church. It would be useless to train these Christians to organize sports clinics for the purpose of reaching out to the rest of the nation with the gospel. Their method would have to be widely different from Christians living in a democratic nation.

No matter what the political and cultural environment is, we have to formulate our methods. We have already covered the method of Christ who selected and developed his disciples and then sent them into the world with the gospel. He trusted them to be faithful in proclaiming and demonstrating the power of the gospel. This example is worthy of imitating, but difficult to put into practice in the 21st century. Since the beginning of modernity in the time of the French Revolution in 1789, the rejection of faith in God has steadily grown among the people of the Western world. The criticism of religion by Karl Marx and the philosophical rejection of the existence of God by Friedrich Nietzsche, encouraged millions of people to believe they became the real gods here on the planet earth. To them faith in God and the presence of his church belong to the past century. To convince these secular people of the love of God for them and his plans with them is an enormous task. By now we have to admit that mere proclamation will not do. God's method is still his men and women. But in our impersonal world, making disciples will not happen without establishing a platform that will give us a new chance to convince the unchurched that they are missing the most vital need of all people, namely a relationship with the eternal God. If we represent our God as joyfully and powerfully as the early disciples did, we will have an opportunity to change their minds from unbelief to a desire to know our God.

There are many methods that Christians use to fulfill the Great Commission. Here is a list of those that are not quite effective:

> Tract distribution, door-to-door visitation, television programs, newspaper advertising, evangelistic crusades, Christian schools, Christian magazines, bus ministry, literacy classes, church surveys, billboards, and revival meetings.

I am not saying that we should do away with these methods and activities, but I claim that they do not really connect us, for whatever reason, with the secular people. Understanding the culture better will move us in a different direction. Here is a list of methods that are more attractive to unbelievers:

> DVD distribution, chat rooms, medical help, summer camping programs, sports clinics, sports banquets, sports competition, recreation centers open to the community, home bible studies, crisis centers, English as a second language classes, disaster relief, and free lunches for the poor.

Notice that these events are for the unchurched. They are possible because Christians are willing to go out of their sanctuaries and make disciples. They depend on the needs in a community and on the resources of the local church. Most of them will work if they are evaluated periodically, adjusted often, and improved in search for better results.

GOALS FOR SPORTS EVANGELISM

Purposes, strategies, and methods will not lead into proper action unless we set goals. Dayton defines a goal, "as a measurable and (in the mind of the person setting it) accomplishable future event. It is measurable both by time (when it will become a past event) and by performance (how we know it has happened)."[22] This definition clearly separates a purpose from a goal. Our purpose for sports evangelism stated in this book is to give glory to God through proclaiming the gospel to the ends of the earth while using sports as the common ground. In this statement we describe the 'why' which is to give God the glory through our proclamation, and the 'what' which is using sports as the common ground. Although we can understand this statement, there is no measurable goal in it, except the rather general notion of the ends of the earth. Looking at this purpose immediately raises the question how are we going to measure our efforts and how are we going to know what we accomplished?

For instance, "to use sports evangelism to share Christ with sports minded people of America" is a statement of purpose. "To equip 50 sports evangelists who will do sports evangelism in all 50 States in the United States of America" is a measurable goal. Is it too presumptuous to set clear-cut goals in the work of a Christian minister or a Christian organization? James knew that setting goals was a statement of faith, but he was not against those goals as long as they were formulated within the will of God, "Now listen, you who say, 'Today or tomorrow we will go to this or that city, spend a year there, carry on business and make money.' Why, you do not even know what will happen tomorrow. What is your life? You are a mist that appears for a little while and than vanishes. Instead, you ought to say, 'If it is the Lord's will, we will live and do this or that'" (James 4:13-15). Paul was not quite sure that he would go all the way to Spain, but he was not afraid to state it as his goal. He desired to proclaim the gospel beyond Rome and Spain was the place to do it. He even asked for help from the Roman believers so that he could realize that goal, "But now that there is no more place for me to work in these regions, and since I have been longing for many years to see you, I plan to do so when I go to Spain. I hope to visit you while passing through and to have you assist me on my journey there, after I have enjoyed your company for a while" (Romans 15:23-24). Paul's purpose was to proclaim the gospel because it was the power of God for the salvation of everyone who believed. Such a purpose was a great motivation for him to keep on doing it. But his goals propelled him to ever new accomplishments. His best statement about pressing toward the ultimate goal is in Phil. 3:12-14, "Not that I have already obtained all this, or have already been made perfect, but I press on to take hold of that for which Christ Jesus took hold of me. Brothers, I do not consider myself yet to have taken hold of it. But one thing I do: Forgetting what is behind and straining toward what is ahead, I press on toward the goal to win the prize for which God called me heavenward in Christ Jesus." Paul was a conqueror. His goals were ever present before him and he pursued them with passion.

Setting goals for sports evangelism

Most Christians will not have a problem accepting the purpose for sports evangelism. They want to proclaim the gospel and can see the validity of using sports as the common ground to relate to the unchurched. The difficulty will arise when a leader in this area will try to set specific goals. No more general statements, but clear and measurable goals. To reach these goals, Christians who agree with using sports evangelism, must spring into action. Any expert on church growth knows that 80% of our people are spectators who think that ministry is just for the paid staff and the lay people who want to work of their own volition. Sports evangelism can provide the motivation for spectators to finally decide to get involved and obey the Great Commission. Specific and measurable goals sold to the congregation will make the difference.

All people have conscious and subconscious goals. Without goals we would not accomplish anything. We set goals for each day. They are there when we wake up – washing our faces, eating breakfast, going to work, buying food, relating to the members of our families, recreating, pursuing hobbies, going to church services, and finally going to sleep to begin the whole process next day.

Maslow describes a hierarchy of needs that forces us to formulate goals – physiological, safety and security, belongingness and love, esteem, and self-actualization.[23] The basic human need is physiological. We must drink and eat to stay alive. In the United States people have clean water to drink and plenty of food to nourish their bodies. The second need for safety and security is ever present in lives of people who venture out of their homes to work and to provide for their families. But once these two basic needs are met, our attention can turn toward the higher needs of Maslow's hierarchy.

In the Western world people are released from the lower needs, even if not completely, to pursue the higher needs of belonging, of esteem, and of self-actualization. Knowing this progression helps us with setting goals for sports evangelism along these lines. Engaging in sports opens people up to belonging to a group of athletes with the same interest. Their desire for affectionate relations will grow as they attain a place within the group. Once they improve in the performance of a given sport, they feel better about themselves and enjoy the esteem of others. This in turn leads to self-confidence, strength, and adequacy. The final need is for self-actualization. If we fail to provide constructively for this need, discontent and restlessness will follow. Maslow claims that self-actualization "refers to man's desire for self-fulfillment, namely, to the tendency for him to become actualized in what he is potentially. This tendency might be phrased as the desire to become more and more what one is, to become everything that one is capable of becoming. The specific form that these needs will take will of course vary greatly from person to person. In one individual it may take the form of the desire to be an ideal mother, in another it may be expressed athletically, and in still another it may be expressed in painting pictures or in inventions."[24] Notice that Maslow mentions the possibility that self-actualization can be accomplished in the athletic world.

Sports evangelism can address all five needs to the satisfaction of participants. Sports events should always include hospitality through offering water and food. Athletes need to be hydrated and nourished especially during physically demanding sports events. Safety and security is a big concern for sports events. When parents trust us with their children to teach them a new sport, our facilities must be up to par with safety regulations. We do not want any accidents that would prevent us from organizing future events. The next need of belongingness and love should be easily met by Christians who desire to love all people. Our environment should be saturated by the spirit of kindness and acceptance. Hopefully, participants will know that this kind of atmosphere is genuine and that they can be at ease among Christians. This is very important in case of an ongoing competition as the secular people join us in a league. The fourth need is esteem. Our individualistic culture does not offer a lot of help in this area. We live in a competitive world where the weaker human beings are left behind. What an opportunity for Christians to correct this unfortunate situation. One way of doing it is through encouragement. I noticed that people will make faster progress in learning a sport when the coach praises them for even the smallest progress. Phrases like, “This was a great shot”, “You can do it”, “Try it again”, “Great effort”, and “You are getting better all the time”, will increase a feeling of self-worth, and esteem. Barnabas was good at encouraging Saul. He gave him a chance to become the best missionary ever even though the apostles in Jerusalem did not want to have anything to do with him because of his persecution of Christians. We will meet people while doing sports evangelism that will not fit our preconceived ideas of doing evangelism. But these are the people that God will send our way to touch their lives and to help them with building up their confidence to face life courageously.

The final need is self-actualization. How can we create an environment that would help secular people to achieve their potential? First, we have to get to know them. They have to trust us to reveal their intimate thoughts to us. Then we have to gently point them toward our Savior Jesus Christ. That will mean that some of their dreams about self-actualization might change by considering eternal values. Our sports goals have to include the possibility of the work of the Holy Spirit that can accomplish the highest achievement of any person in the area of self-actualization by becoming mature in Jesus Christ. Paul experienced the beauty of this self-actualization when he claimed, "I can do everything through him who gives me strength" (Philippians 4:13).

Our knowledge of five basic needs of human beings is not enough to formulate our goals clearly. Another aspect of this process is to understand a given culture where we are going to do sports evangelism. The scope of this book doesn't allow for an extensive analysis of different cultures, but a short contextualization of the Western culture will serve as an example of taking seriously our approach to reach our own people. North America, Europe, and Australia have become a mission field through massive secularization. Now Christians have the task of winning their peoples to Christ again. Hunter defines six watershed events that led to Christendom's decline over six centuries: the Renaissance, the Protestant Reformation, Nationalism, the rise of Science, the Enlightenment, and Urbanization.[25] The volcanic event that brought the secular and atheistic ideas to the forefront of especially European nations was the French Revolution in 1789.

The ideas of Nietzsche, Freud, Darwin, and Marx spread like wildfire, but the church continued as if the cultural landscape remained the same with the exception of scientific discoveries that shed new light on the universe we live in. The

Copernican revolution dismissed the three-storied universe and the church had to adjust its creeds. But the church did not do sufficient contextualization to figure out how to relate to this new breed of people who rejected Christianity and started to believe that every religion has some truth within its teachings and that each person can pick and choose what he wants to believe. Because of this lack of interaction between the church and the secular people, Christianity surrendered its public influence for the existence in a ghetto of a private spiritual sector. The church is still in the world, but because of its fear not to become of the world, it hides behind the walls of sanctuaries and private church organizations. The Great Commission doesn't allow for this kind of abdication of our accountability before our Savior Jesus Christ.

Is the progress of secularization an insurmountable obstacle for Christians to live their lives in the public square? According to Hunter, Christians faced similar problems in the first century.

> For the Christian movement's first three centuries, the communication of Christianity had to achieve four objectives: (1) Facing a population with no knowledge of the gospel, the Christian movement had to inform people of the story of Jesus, the good news,

its claims, and its offer. (2) Facing hostile populations and persecution of the state, the Church had to 'win friends and influence people' to a positive attitude toward the movement. (3) Facing an Empire with several entrenched religions, the Christians had to convince people of Christianity's truth, or at least of its plausibility. (4) Since entry into the faith is an act of the will, Christians had to invite people to adopt this faith and join the messianic community and follow Jesus as Lord. These were the components of persuasion in the ancient setting. The early church was intentional about achieving each of these four objectives. They informed people by creatively communicating and interpreting their gospel in conversations, synagogue presentations, and open-air speaking. They influenced people's attitudes by their changed lives, their ministries of service, their love for one another, and by their love for nonchristians and even their enemies, even in martyrdom. They convinced people by reasoning from the Scriptures and by their common-sense apologetics. They invited responsive people to confess faith and be baptized into the messianic community. [26]

Our situation is similar, yet different. We have the same objectives, but not the same people.

The secular people of the 21st century, especially in the Western world, have been influenced by a critical attitude toward Christianity. Our first task is then to 'win friends and influence people' and to enable them to have faith in Jesus Christ and eventually to join the church because Christianity is not a solitary religion. The first century culture did not have the luxury of much free time to devote to sports. But our culture is sports crazy and ready to open up to Christians who have contextualized their evangelistic zeal. To use the analogy of a farmer working in the field, we must prepare the spoiled soil, scatter the seed, water, and finally gather the harvest. The field is not ours anymore. It belongs predominantly to the enemy who would like to silence us in the name of tolerance and pluralism. Just as the early Christians, we must enter the world stage again one by one and be intentional in stating and reaching our goals.

Measurable and accomplishable goals

Goals that can motivate must be stated clearly. Time and performance are two categories that will determine our success in reaching goals. Time will show us whether we estimated adequate length of time to make the goal a past event.

Performance will determine the quality of our effort and the fruit of our work. In a church setting the first goal must deal with the communication of the importance of embarking on a new way of doing evangelism. The pastor must be able to create a genuine interest in doing sports evangelism. How does he know if he succeeds? He should preach on the need of reaching the community for Christ and give an invitation to those interested to join him in a seminar on sports evangelism. He can teach the seminar himself or he can invite a sports evangelist. The initial goal should be twofold: preach two successive sermons on the subject of sports evangelism during first two Sundays in April and offer a seminar on sports evangelism on the first Saturday in May. When this goal is accomplished, the church should offer the first sports evangelistic clinic in July. The leader will have enough time to train his workers (May), give out invitations in the community (June and July), ask the members of the church to pray for God's blessings upon that event (May-July), and have time left during summer to do proper follow up (July-August). This goal is measurable and accomplishable. Notice that I did not include the number of workers and the number of participants. The first attempt is hard to predict. High numbers might not happen and, therefore, discourage the church as a whole. Low numbers would show low expectation and could prevent some people from participation. The very first attempt at sports evangelism should be done no matter what the results. The adjustments and improvements can easily follow. The second round of training and of the sports clinic should be done September through November. The community will notice when a church is serious about extending a ministry and keeping on doing it for the benefit of the people living around the church.

When I pastored a church of 45 members, I put a sports clinic on the yearly calendar. I did not know what to expect, but I trained 5 people, advertized it in and around the church, and I prayed. We offered teaching of tennis, football, and softball on Saturday from 9 to 12. I was a little bit disappointed when only 15 children came. We did our drills in our parking lot and on a softball field and everybody seemed to have a good time. Some parents stayed around and watched what we were doing. During the break, we were able to meet them and tell them why we were offering a sports clinic. They were quite pleased that a church was reaching their kids with wholesome activity. I reserved the last 30 minutes for reward presentations for those children who did exceptionally well. Then I shared the gospel and gave an invitation. One boy accepted Christ as his Savior. I baptized him two months later. He and his grandmother became members of our church and are faithful to the Lord. In fact, I repented of my initial feelings of disappointment. At the end of the clinic I had reasons to praise God for allowing me to reach one youth with the gospel.

Participation in a clinic depends on the size of a congregation and on the makeup of the community. But we should not be hesitant to start small. If a church can mobilize 10% of its members to be involved in sports evangelism, it is a good start. Remember what Jesus did. He selected just 12 men at the beginning of his ministry, invested his life in them, and now Christianity is the only religion present in every nation of our world.

Once the members of a local congregation show enough interest in sports evangelism, the momentum must be sustained by additional goals and events. At this point, three categories of goals will emerge – overall, intermediate, and immediate. The overall goal will deal with the ongoing ministry of sports evangelism as an established method of outreach. The leader will make plans for sports evangelism events every year and will expand them by at least one event yearly. The intermediate goal will call for 5 % increase in volunteer workers every year necessary to keep sports evangelism growing. The goal accompanying the expansion will provide for two training seminars each year guaranteeing the equipping of new workers. The church will have to approve funds suggested by the leader of sports ministry and include them in the yearly budget to pay for expenses associated with the ongoing ministry. The immediate goals can be quite a few depending upon the situation of the state of sports evangelism in a given church. Here are some examples of goals demanding immediate attention for staging a sports clinic in a local church:

- Praying for God's blessing upon the sports clinic every day (May-July)
- Preaching sermons on the need to get involved in sports evangelism (May)
- Offering a sports evangelism seminar in June
- Signing up 15 church members for the seminar (May)
- Setting the date for a sports clinic in July
- Getting a permission to use a public facility (June)
- Providing a sports facility at the church - a parking lot might do (June)
- Asking 5 church members with sports background to coach (June)
- Asking 3 church members to be referees (June)

- Advertizing the sports clinic in a local newspaper and a radio station (June-July)
- Securing 3 sponsors (June-July)
- Asking 5 church members to prepare refreshments (June)
- Buying 2 rewards for each sport taught (June)
- Reserving 30 minutes for the conclusion of the sports clinic (July)
- Choosing 1 person to present the gospel (July)
- Having 4 counselors to clarify decisions people make (July)
- Contacting all participants by a personal call and a letter (August)
- Evaluating the clinic and planning the next event for the glory of God (August).

The first sports clinic will bring new insights and future possibilities. Adjusting goals is part of the process that will continually improve our efforts. There should be no hesitancy to review honestly and to plan courageously based on our evaluation and experience in our setting. Now we are ready to proceed to uncover the many possibilities of doing sports evangelism.

CHAPTER SIX

DOING SPORTS EVANGELISM

The year was 1996 when I watched the final match of the French Open. Michael Chang beat Stefan Edberg 6-1, 3-6, 4-6, 6-4, 6-2 and the people in the stands waited patiently to hear him speak. As he was receiving the trophy for his win, he pulled a paper from his back pocket and began reading. Here are his words: "I thank the Lord Jesus Christ because without him, I am nothing." Spectators in the stadium and those who watched him on TV throughout the world heard this courageous testimony. Michael was giving Jesus the glory for his accomplishment. He became the youngest-ever male player to win a Grand Slam singles tennis title at the age of 17.

Win or lose, Michael honors God by his attitude and his testimony. He thanks God for giving him the talent to play tennis. He continues speaking up for God, "People forget great shots and great victories. But if you touch a person's life for Christ, it stays with them for a lifetime. The platform I have through tennis is a wonderful opportunity to make a difference in people's lives." Currently Michael sponsors a number of ministerial sporting events including Christian sports leagues and worldwide tennis camps. He is doing sports evangelism on a large scale that reaches Christians and non-Christians. The Chang Family Foundation tries to reach people who love sports but do not go to church. Through different competitions, these athletes are introduced to churches and to Christ. Christian athletes, professional or amateur, should imitate an example of Michael Chang. The Lord can give us platforms that will reach people with the gospel. The field is open for those who will take the step of faith and do evangelism in obedience to the Great Commission.

The persisting problem in Western Christianity is the inactivity of the majority of church members who limit their church life to a Sunday morning worship service. To get these Christians from the pews to interact with the secular people is a great task. We have no other option if we want to live up to Peter's assessment of Christians as 'the royal priesthood'. Those who read his first letter agreed with him and joined the apostles in becoming informal witnesses of Jesus Christ.

But the fire of spreading the gospel message went out in later centuries. Luther, after studying the letter to the Romans, spoke about the need for the priesthood of all believers as part of his proposed reformation. Our century has to hear again this call for laity to take seriously their responsibility to reach our world with the Good News. One way to hear this call among the laity is to define ministries they can do and challenge them to get involved. I am convinced that the ministry of sports evangelism fits the picture splendidly. Since 96% of all people are interested in sports directly or indirectly, we can mobilize, equip, and deploy this vast number of people to work in the Kingdom of God.

The prevalent way of doing evangelism is the evangelistic-attractional mode. Attracting people through special events to visit a local church has worked for many years. Some church growth happened, especially in mega churches, and so the method is still taught in church growth seminars. Pastors that learn and apply this evangelistic-attractional approach see mixed results. Church growth statistics reveal that 80% of all churches in America are plateaued and declining. There must be a better way to do evangelism so that these churches can become comeback churches that are leaving the ranks of declining congregations. Hirsch proposes that we need to link two practices together – missional and incarnational, "The missional-incarnational impulse is, in effect, the practical outworking of the mission of God (the *mission Dei*) and of the incarnation. It is thus rooted in the very way that God has redeemed the world, and in how God revealed himself to us."[1] The incarnation of Jesus Christ is a shining example for us to follow. We are to live in the midst of our culture for the sake of impacting the people around us. The missional aspect of evangelism draws its inspiration from the work that God initiates and sustains in the world. We are to become God's partners offering redemption to all people and planting churches among them. The early church was much more missional-incarnational than evangelistic-attractional. There were very few attractive events the church would organize. Those events that would qualify would be meetings where people were healed by the power of Jesus Christ. But these meetings happened for the sake of proclaiming the gospel first. The signs and wonders were a byproduct of the power of God and the faith of the early disciples.

Planning sports evangelism will include some attractive events. Organizing clinics, leagues, tournaments, and camps will give us a unique opportunity to get out of our sanctuaries and be missional-incarnational. Why is it that we do not see enough of this approach happening? One reason is that church members are not accustomed to step out on the secular stage as bold witnesses for Christ. It is so much easier to attract non-Christians to come to us and see what we are doing. However, there are too few people who will come on our turf. Research confirms that 95% of the unchurched will not visit a church of their own volition. We have to be incarnational by meeting them in the secular setting and gain their trust. Hunter makes us aware of the credibility factor when he writes, "But credibility involves more than genuine personal faith. The Church is rightly haunted by Nietzsche's challenge: 'I shall not believe in the redeemer of these Christians until they show me they are redeemed.' Ralph Waldo Emerson observed that 'the reason why anyone refuses his assent to your opinion, or his aid to your benevolent design, is in you. He refuses to accept you as bringer of truth, because, though you think you have it, he feels you have it not. You have not given him the authentic sign.'"[2] The world around us is watching us and comparing our lives with theirs. If we want a platform from which to address non-Christians, we have to give them the authentic sign of true Christian living in a secular culture.

Another reason for our hesitancy to address our secular culture is our uncertainty about the best course of action. Blackaby and King wrote a popular book in 1990 they called

Experiencing God. They encouraged their readers, "Watch to see where God is working and join him."[3] In spite of the widespread usage of this teaching material in Southern Baptist churches, there was no significant increase of mobilization of church members to enter the ranks of intentional witnesses representing God in the world. Left up to the subjective evaluation of an average Christian, the conclusion can be made that God is not working in my place and so I can stay inactive till the situation changes. This attitude puts Christians at ease that is not biblical. God is omnipresent and he is actively seeking the redemption of all people. Therefore, we must accept a task from God in any and every place no matter what our perception is. Downs evaluates the same idea, "The problem we face today is that the average, action-oriented evangelical, seeking to know and do the will of God, often goes through a thought process like this: *To do the will of God, I must find out where God is working and join Him there. Nothing seems to be happening here, but there's plenty of action over there. Obviously, God is at work over there, so that's where I must go to join Him*....My concern is that we've come to believe that God is *more* at work in these places- *more at work in harvesting than in sowing*."[4]

Fifty years ago we could count on a general knowledge of the gospel in America. Harvesting was relatively simple in a predominantly Christian culture. The 21st century is a post-Christian culture where churches are dying. Malphurs claims that there are approximately 350,000 churches in America. He cites an article that, "predicts that in the next few years 100,000 of these churches will close their doors. Consequently, at least a third or more of today's churches did not survive the 1990's."[5] We do not have the luxury of waiting around and hoping that our culture will change. The time is overdue when we must enter the world and make our presence count. Here is a good example of a group of Christians penetrating the secular culture in Australia:

> The story is that of Third Place Communities (TPC), a mission agency that was set up to incarnate Jesus communities in *third places*. For those who are unaware of the term, our first place is the home, our second place is work/school, and our third place is where we spend our time when we have time off. Anywhere people gather for social reasons could be a good place for missional engagement. Third places are pubs, cafes, hobby clubs, sports centers, etc. For these communities "church" takes place wher-ever they are. Through this approach TPC has made a significant impact on Hobart (Australia) just by

hanging out and being the people of God in public spaces. The vast majority of the people who hang out with them are very inquisitive non-Christians. TPC is now in its fourth year of mission. These are still early days, and they feel that they have just started to find their groove and move more closely into their sense of calling, but they recognize that they are in it for the long haul. Being involved incarnationally has meant the members of the community have been transformed into genuine missionaries to their city. In just over three years, they have found themselves profoundly connected with a large range of people in the broader (non-Christian) community. Many of these relationships have become deep and intimate as over this period they experienced life together through the celebration of engagements, weddings, birthdays, births, and life in general. Their missional rhythms include weekly hospitality around tables, serving the community together, raising money for those in need, enjoying and sponsoring local art and music, burying loved ones, sharing ideas about life, praying together, and exploring the stories about Jesus in the context of life. They have seen some come to active faith in Jesus, and many others are close to it.

> Some are of course still exploring, and still others just love being part of the community and are involved at deep levels but are content not to explore it further at this stage. But for all of these people, whether they realize it or not, Jesus now inhabits their worlds in ways they are meaningful and tangible. Now when they think about themselves, the world around them, or their work or play, Jesus is part of the equation, where he was not before.[6]

The missional-incarnational approach to evangelism is happening. And even more so, it is possible. Hirsch mentions sports centers as places for TPC ministry, but doesn't elaborate on the activities happening there. I will describe the whole spectrum of sports evangelism activities available to Christians who would like to get involved in this ministry.

PLANNING FOR SPORTS EVANGELISM

The best way to contemplate the future is to remember how we got to this point. We stated our purpose as giving glory to God through proclaiming the gospel to the ends of the earth while using sports as the common ground. Then we defined strategy as an overall approach, plan, or way of describing how we will go about reaching our goal or solving our problem. We presented a grand strategy, an intermediate strategy, and a short-range strategy with the warning that we should not allow any strategy to become fossilized. The next step was the reminder that we needed a method that would guide us in doing sports evangelism in a regular and orderly way. Jesus showed us his method by training and using men that would reach all nations with the Good News. Finally, we were ready to write about goals as measurable and accomplishable future events.

Since our purpose is to actually do sports evangelism, we must proceed. If we stopped here, we would be like a traveler who got off the train before its final destination. So, planning, acting, and evaluating are the only way to fulfill the command of Christ to go unto all nations. Dayton advices that, "Planning should be thought of as a bridge between where we are now and the future we believe God desires for us. It is true that planning usually includes a series of well-thought-out steps of how we will proceed in order to achieve our goal. What people often fail to see, however, is that plans for people need to be revised continually. We take first step forward, look backward, look forward, and then plan again as necessary. Planning is an attempt to produce surprise-free futures, to anticipate as much as possible what the future is likely to hold and how we will respond to it."[7] We will do our planning from the perspective of a local church because that is where our workers are. They might not be mobilized as yet, but it is the church members who are the main resource for accomplishing our mission. These are the planning steps a church should take to establish a ministry of sports evangelism:

- Form a prayer group that would agree to ask God's blessings on the new venture of the church to reach sports minded people. Ask them to pray for God's guidance in this endeavor and God's blessing on everyone involved in this evangelistic outreach.
- Select a leader that is qualified spiritually and athletically. There is an immediate need for a point man. Someone who envisions sports evangelism to become an integral part of the life of the church. Be careful not to select a man who would just like to get more exposure and prominence in the church. The leader will have a tough task to mobilize, energize, equip, and encourage workers.
- Publicize the possibility of sports evangelism ministry throughout the church. The pastor should announce the ministry from the pulpit and write

about it in his monthly newsletter. Staff people should prepare posters and place them in strategic places in the church.

- Evaluate facilities in the church. If there are none, ask about the availability of public facilities in the city. Using public fields, stadiums, and clubs will give the church a greater exposure in the community.
- Ask for funds coming from the budget of the church. Any new ministry demands financial support. Plans that lack finances usually do not come true.
- Offer a sports evangelism conference. There are qualified speakers whose expertise is in the area of sports ministry. Bringing a specialist will create a greater interest in sports evangelism especially if you can ask a known athlete who proved himself as an ambassador for Christ in the area of sports. The first seminar could last one day to attract as many Christians as possible.
- Recruit the workers. Selection is better than an open call. The leader has knowledge of church members and should use it for consideration of like-minded Christians. Quality is more important than quantity.
- Train the workers. They should agree on the purpose, strategies, methods, goals, and plans of sports

ministry. In order to act as professionals, they should go through a sports clinic organized just for the members of the church. They must not ever look as if they do not know what they are doing. Remember that we do sports evangelism for the glory of God. This fact alone should produce the very best effort.

- Publicize every event throughout your community at least three times. You want all people to have a chance to decide to come and participate in the outreach of the church. Your local paper and the radio station are good possibilities. Going through your community and giving invitations personally will impress the people even more. A big poster in front of the church on a busy street will catch the attention of drivers especially if they see the poster each day for two weeks.
- Join city leagues. There is no substitute for penetrating the secular culture in its own backyard. Ask your members to be on their best behavior while interacting with athletes in the public arena. What a chance to prove a better lifestyle to those who might not be able to control their emotions during a competitive sport event.

- Use major sports events like the Super Bowl, the Daytona 500 car race, the World Cup in soccer, Wimbledon tournament, and the Olympic Games to come to church to watch and to enjoy refreshments.
- Follow up on any of these activities by writing a letter of appreciation. It takes about seven touches from a Christian to establish communication and credibility with the unchurched.
- Express thanks to every worker in sports evangelism after each event and organize a banquet yearly to form a spirit of solidarity among sports evangelists. Testimonies of God's work in the lives of participants can encourage workers to persevere in doing sports evangelism.
- Evangelize, evangelize, and evangelize. Planning for sports evangelism should result in actual witnessing. I am aware of the fact that in our culture we need to prepare the hearts of our friends and that we have to take time to sow the seeds of the gospel in their minds. But we must never lose sight of our ultimate objective to proclaim the Good News with the goal of presenting the opportunity to nonbelievers to believe in our Savior Jesus Christ.

SPORTS EVANGELISM ACTIVITIES

The most important activity in sports evangelism is the going and making disciples. If we did witnessing among sports minded people on every day basis, this section would not have to be written. We would be intentional in forming relationships and in seeking the best opportunities to lead people to Christ. The method of Jesus was Christians sharing with those who still did not know him. But since the great majority of Christians are not faithful in presenting Christ now, we must plan, delegate, and supervise the most important ministry of the church. What follows are activities and events in sports evangelism that will hopefully draw many Christians into intentional witnessing.

Sports evangelism conference

The initial attempt to start sports evangelism in a church must be continually reinforced by publicity, testimonies, and proper events. The first event should be a sports evangelism conference for interested members of the church. The leader in this area chooses the date, the speaker, and the place where the conference will happen. He will need a hall where the participants can study, eat, and fellowship. Here is an example of a one-day conference:

SCHEDULE OF A ONE-DAY SPORTS EVANGELISM CONFERENCE

Saturday

9:30 – 10:00 am	Registration and snacks
10:00 – 10:15am	Welcome
10:15 – 11:15 am	Introduction of Christianity and Sports
11:15 – 11:30 am	Break
11:30 – 12:30 pm	Biblical and Theological Foundations for Sports Evangelism
12:30 – 1:30 pm	Lunch and fellowship
1:30 – 2:30 pm	A Sports Evangelism Witness
2:30 – 2:45 pm	Break
2:45 – 3:45 pm	Purposes, strategies, methods, and goals for Sports Evangelism
3:45 – 4:00 pm	Break
4:00 – 5:00 pm	Doing Sports Evangelism
5:00 – 5:15 pm	Questions/Answers/ Concluding prayers

The one-day conference can be easily expanded to one and a half day. This conference should include a demonstration of a sports clinic.

EVANGELISM CONFERENCE

Friday

5:00 – 5:30 pm	Registration and snacks
5:30 – 6:30 pm	Introduction of Christianity and Sports
6:30 – 7:30 pm	Dinner and fellowship
7:30 – 8:30 pm	Biblical and Theological foundations of Sports Evangelism
8:30 – 8:45 pm	Questions/Answers/ Concluding prayers

Saturday

9:30 – 9:45 am	Snacks and fellowship
9:45 – 10:45 am	A Sports Evangelism Witness
10:45 – 11:00 am	Break
11:00 – 12:00 pm	Purposes, strategies, methods, and goals for Sports Evangelism

12:00 – 1:00 pm	Lunch
1:00 – 2:00 pm	Doing Sports Evangelism
2:00 – 2:30 pm	Question/Answers /Prayers
2:30 – 3:00 pm	Moving to a sports facility
3:00 – 4:30 pm	Doing and explaining a sports clinic
4:30 – 5:00 pm	Concluding remarks and prayers

Sports evangelism clinic

Learning about sports evangelism must result in actions. The very first event should be a sports clinic where the volunteers from the church teach different sports. It would help if a prominent professional or a college athlete would coach the participants, but it is not always necessary. Amateurs with sufficient expertise and spiritual preparedness qualify for the job as well. Most parents bringing children to a clinic are not experts themselves, however, they are sensitive to the way how we organize and lead the clinic. Do the children have a good time? Have they learned something new that will encourage them to continue wanting to learn more? Will they want to come to the next sports clinic? These are important questions that the coaches should keep in mind.

The first sports clinic should offer at least two sports. Children are picky and we need to give them choices. If they do not like soccer, they can play baseball. If they are not crazy about baseball, they might want to play basketball. We can possibly increase the number of sports later on as we have more participants and coaches.

TYPES OF SPORTS EVANGELISM CLINICS

- Station to station. Students rotate from station to station to learn more sports than just one. Or they can stay in one station and get further instruction.
- Coaching. Playing sports and coaching are two different activities. Older athletes have the experience necessary for coaching, but they need to learn the art of teaching a sport and forming a team that can win.
- Officiating. There are many amateur leagues that need umpires. A local church can provide basic training for men and women who enjoy officiating.

GOALS FOR SPORTS EVANGELISM CLINICS

- To present the Gospel to all participants. This is the highest goal for the clinic. We have to formulate all other goals from the perspective of introducing participants to Jesus Christ.

- To instruct in two sports. The attractiveness of the clinic is in the promise of learning skills that will help participants to make progress in a given sport. To fulfill that promise, we must offer the best possible instruction that is efficient and enjoyable.
- To provide Christian atmosphere through Christ honoring coaches. Even though it is possible to use a coach who is not a Christian, we must not overlook the fact that the people from the community are observing us and expect certain level of attractive behavior. All coaches and personnel should agree to represent Christ through teaching and relating to participants.
- To make participants welcome by showing the love of Christ to them. There will be instances when instructors might get angry with students who do not follow prescribed guidelines. There is a place for strict instruction, but at the same time it must be done in a kind and loving manner. Where else can the participant expect a community of people who love one another in spite of our shortcomings? And where else can he taste the Christian fellowship?

- To facilitate an interaction with the community on the church's grounds. One of the toughest tasks a church is facing today is to bring people to church. Secular people drive by many church buildings, but have no desire to come in. As if the church no longer provided what people want and need. When we offer a sports evangelism clinic in the church, they come because of the instruction, not because they would suddenly want to attend a church service. Once they are in the church facility, we have a unique opportunity to convince them that they are missing something they cannot find anywhere else.
- To follow up by contacting every participant within a week. It takes about seven positive touches before a secular person will change his negative opinion about Christians or the church as a whole. A friendly follow up visit with people who had a good experience during the clinic, will keep the door open for future participation or presentation of the Good News. Coaches, instructors, and counselors should take part in this effort because they have already established a relationship with participants and possibly with their parents or relatives.

SETTING A BUDGET FOR SPORTS EVANGELISM CLINICS

Sports evangelism clinics cost money. A detailed budget must be in place at the very beginning of planning. A local church might put the expense for a clinic into the yearly budget, or the money can come from private donations and sponsors.

- Gifts for instructors. Offering some money to instructors who will spend time and energy to prepare and to execute an effective teaching, should be done. If they refuse to accept the money, then there will be funds for additional improvements in different areas.
- Refreshments. Students get hungry and thirsty while playing sports. Drinks and food should be available at appropriate times. These breaks give us a better opportunity to get to know the participants and to establish better relationships.
- Awards. Everybody likes to win. Awards given at the end of the clinic recognize the best improved player, the most skilled player, and the most likeable player. The joy expressed on the faces of those who receive

awards, is worth every dollar spent for those trophies, or just certificates.

- Equipment. Not all children come to the clinic with their equipment. Some of them want to learn a sport they have never played before, so we cannot expect them to come fully equipped. But equipment can be costly. Probably the best way to provide for the participants is to ask sporting goods shops for donations. You will be surprised how many managers of stores with sports equipment will give their merchandise for this occasion. Or you can buy some of the equipment and receive the rest of it free of charge.
- Transportation. There will be children who will want to attend a clinic, but will have no ride. Volunteers from the church should be able to pick those children up and bring them to the facility. Or if your church owns a van, someone from the church can pick up more children from your neighborhood. This offer will ensure a greater number of participants for the clinic.
- Publicity. In order to have many people to come to the clinic, they have to know about it. Church members can place posters and fliers in local shops. Some radio and TV stations offer free announcements for

community events. Advertising in a local newspaper is still effective, but do not forget the internet if your church has a webpage.

- Participants' fees. One way to cover your expenses is to charge a small fee. The fee should be small in order not to exclude children who have a hard time to come up with the money. But a fee is appropriate because of the expenses associated with the clinic. People who paid a fee will show up more readily than those who did not.
- Facility fees. It is better to pay for a good facility than to offer a substandard place. There are many sport facilities that are excellent and churches should use them to make a good impression on the participants. You cannot provide a great instruction on a field that is not built for that particular sport. Teaching baseball demands a baseball field and teaching tennis demands a tennis court. Without the proper facility, you have to improvise and the impression is less than satisfactory.

REGISTRATION FOR SPORTS EVANGELISM CLINICS

Registration is vital for the future ministry among participants. The best way to register everyone is on the internet. There you will communicate the most important information including the deadline and the registration fee. There is no paperwork. There are no delays allowed. The number of participants is known because of a due date and planning can be completed on time. If you do not have a webpage, then you have to provide registration forms administered by a secretary. Here is the necessary information for each student:

- Name – first and last.
- Address. This is an important data to determine whether the student lives in a close proximity to the church.
- Telephone numbers – both home and cell phone numbers.
- Emergency contact. In case of an accident, the parent should know about it within minutes. There should be no negligence on your part to communicate with the family of the student.
- Allergies, special needs, bee stings, medications. Prevention of unexpected happenings is a must during a clinic at the church. Knowing about possible problems will expedite necessary steps.

- Parental consent. It is absolutely necessary to have a signature of the parent on the registration form to agree to the participation of his child in the clinic. This consent will protect the church from a possible lawsuit.
- Preference of sport (baseball, basketball, football, tennis, golf, etc). In a station to station clinic it helps when the director knows the number of participants for each sport. If the facility doesn't allow for a bigger group in one sport, adjustments must be made before the beginning of the clinic.
- Liability waiver. You can count on the fact that some unforeseen things will be happening. Therefore, a liability waiver should be signed by parents when they bring their children to participate in church clinic. Here is a statement that will protect a church from being sued when accidents occur:

  "I, the undersigned parent/guardian of the student named above, hereby waive any right that I, or said minor child, may have to sue Community Church or any other employees and volunteers, as a result of any and all injuries, damages, or losses sustained by the student while participating in the sports evangelism clinic."
- Signature and date.

SELECTING A SITE

Many small churches do not have adequate facility to host a clinic. This fact, however, should not keep them from offering a clinic to their neighborhood. There are public parks, schools, and stadiums available for a fee. The advantage of organizing a sports evangelism clinic on a neutral ground is the exposure a church can have by leaving its facility and meeting people in places they enjoy on a continual basis. If no facility is available for a particular date, there is a possibility to do this outreach with a larger church that has a field, a court, or a Family Life Center that would provide for an ideal facility. Cooperation, rather than competition among churches, should be in place since we are trying to do the same outreach. Here are some things to consider before choosing a site.

- Accessibility. The facility should be readily accessible and known in the community. There is no reason for people not to be able to follow directions, or even to get lost in a maze of streets leading to the clinic's field.
- Attractiveness. It is better to pay a higher fee to reserve an attractive facility, than to get a place that

is filthy, in disrepair, and not really suitable for an enjoyable time for all participants. A visit to the area before the actual clinic will help determine whether the facility will serve you well or not.

- Restrooms. A clinic that lasts more than two hours should include a restroom facility. There is nothing worse than to have to drive students away from the facility to use a restroom. They will miss valuable instruction and will disrupt the smooth flow of the clinic.
- Safety. If the facility is not maintained on regular basis, there might be accidents waiting to happen – holes in the ground, slick spots after the rain, no protection from the sun or rain. These issues must be taken into consideration because the safety of the participants must come first.
- Size. Overcrowding can be detrimental to the success of the clinic. Knowing the size of the facility will determine the number of participants. If the interest is high, which usually doesn't happen during the very first clinic, some students have to be turned down. You can do it politely by offering them another date for the same type of clinic. This is a much better option than to deal with students whose time seems

wasted as they wait for their turn to put into practice what the instructor wants them to learn.

SELECTING A TIME

Time makes a difference in the attendance of the clinic. The first clinic should not be longer than three hours. Students like to keep on moving and learning at a fast pace that is easily sustainable in a shorter period of time. Saturday morning is probably the best time to have parents bring their children to the clinic. Here is a schedule for the first clinic that will enable the church to achieve its goals:

9:00	-	10:00	Prayer and preparation
10:00	-	10:15	Registration
10:15	-	10:45	First session teaching soccer and baseball
10:45	-	10:50	Change stations
10:50	-	11:00	Refreshments
11:00	-	11:30	Second session teaching baseball and soccer
11:30	-	11:45	Gospel presentation
11:45	-	12:00	Awards ceremony

Sports evangelism leagues

Leagues that are organized by the church for the members of the church do not serve the goal of intentional evangelism. A church team has two options to become involved in reaching out to secular people. First, players on the team can decide to invite secular people to play on their team. Then it is fine to continue playing in the church league because outreach will be happening during each game. Second, and this is a better option, the church team could join a city-wide league where Christians have a chance to interact with many people who do not even go to church. One thing is of utmost importance when we enter the secular playing field. We must represent Christ extremely well because the people around us are observing and possibly critiquing our behavior. But what an opportunity to prove to non Christians that we do not have to cuss, argue, cheat, get angry, and be violent when the game doesn't go our way. A behavior like this will raise questions in the minds of secular players. They will eventually want to know the secret of a different way of playing sports. At this point, we can easily speak about our Savior Jesus Christ who equips us to live the abundant life. Some training is necessary so that we do not miss these God-given opportunities to be his witnesses.

Upward Basketball is an organization that took the idea of a league and adjusted it for outreach among children. They are using a ball to invite children to the church. Each season consists of eight games and ten practices with a devotional midway through each practice. Children pay a fee, but scholarships are available for those who need financial assistance.

Caz McCaslin created Upward Basketball in 1986 at his church in Spartanburg, South Carolina. As a recreation minister, he wanted to share Christ through sports with people who have never been to church before. Upward's mission is to introduce children to Jesus Christ by creating opportunities to serve through sports. In eight years the enrollment of children playing basketball in his church grew to more than 700 children. By 1996 this sports ministry spread to sixty-four churches with more than 13,000 children. Because of tremendous growth in the area of basketball, Upward added cheerleading, soccer, and flag football. In 2007 489,580 children participated in Upward. Based on decision cards returned to Upward from participating churches, the average number of children saved per church was twenty-two.

Sports evangelism tournaments

Tournaments last two or three days. Players sign up and look forward to the competition that will produce a winner.

All players hope to reach the final round and to win the title, but only one will make it. No matter who wins the first prize, Christians can impress visiting players of the beauty of living the purposeful life that only Christ can offer.

There are tournaments for individuals like tennis and golf, and tournaments for teams like soccer, baseball, softball, basketball, and football. These events need quite a few volunteers to oversee day to day scheduling of games and maintaining the facility. To bring a tournament to a successful conclusion is a matter of organizational skill and flexibility that Christians should be able to offer. A good way to conclude a tournament is to invite all players to a final ceremony of giving trophies to winners and runner-ups. Church members have a unique opportunity to get involved in running tournaments and use the playing field for intentional evangelism.

One of my former students,Tim Irwin, is now overseeing the sports outreach ministry at Englewood Baptist Church in Rocky Mount, North Carolina. His objective is to reach children through organizing basketball and soccer tournaments and leagues. The results are amazing. Just in one year the church saw 800 kids playing basketball, 500 involved in soccer, and 400 in baseball. He describes the outreach in these words, "It's a big net. It's one of the biggest nets we throw. I can't think of a larger net." While children are playing competitive sports, coaches and leaders use breaks to teach them from God's word. Parents watching their children will hear testimonies from one of the coaches. This devotional time ends with a prayer.

Additional benefit from tournaments and leagues is the discovery of people who will welcome members of the church in their homes. They met them on the playing field and they are open to their evangelistic visit. Irwin says, "There were 70 to 80 families that didn't list any church (on their application), so man, they go right into our FAITH evangelistic program. We're visiting them from Day One. And we're visiting them again and again. Over the course of a year doing these sports, we've had just hundreds and hundreds of good quality visits. What more can you ask for?" The net is truly large and the results are there. In its eight year history, the recreational ministry at Englewood saw more than 1,000 professions of faith from children and adults who found their way to church through sports.

Tim invited me to speak at Englewood to children and their parents at the end of one of the soccer tournaments. I gave my testimony about living the Christian life as a professional athlete. Tim presented the Gospel and then gave trophies to those who did exceptionally well. There were about 2,000 people gathered in the sanctuary, enjoying themselves and tasting the fellowship of Christians. Sports truly provide a very large net. Irvin leaves us with a challenge, "Why would somebody not want to do something like this. Every church has got a patch of land or access to land or something. Why would you not want to try to do something to reach kids."

Sports evangelism banquets

People like to get together to eat and to be entertained. Banquets, at the end of a league or a tournament, will draw a crowd. The attendance will be even greater if the church can invite a professional athlete who will give his testimony to the glory of God. Known Christian athletes are willing to accept an invitation from a local church if they are asked at least a year ahead of that speaking engagement. So plan the program early and publicize it throughout your community.

There is a very effective sports ministry done for many years among people who like to hunt. Churches have shown cooperation in announcing and preparing banquets for Big Game Dinners where a big game and safari hunter speaks and presents his precious trophies. A popular speaker at these banquets is Dr. Paige Patterson, president of Southwestern Baptist Theological seminary in Fort Worth, Texas. In

September 2003 he drew a crowd of 1,300 men and boys at a rural church near Fort Smith, Arkansas. That was a big turnout for a small town with a population of 1, 800. The goal of the banquet was to get guys see the things in the church that they are usually looking for in the woods on Sunday. But intentional evangelism was the major objective. God blessed this effort by welcoming twenty seven men into his kingdom. Another twenty six men decided to renew their hunting licenses. I hope that some of them will follow the example of Paige Patterson by witnessing about Christ at future big game banquets.

In January 2009, Patterson spoke in a Men's Big Game Dinner in Spencer, Virginia to more than 300 men. One of my former students, Martha Jones, described the event, "Our goal was to reach lost boys and men, so we tried to be intentional about where we placed fliers (hunting stores, convenience stores, local restaurants, newspapers – in the sport section; we did not advertise to local churches). We offered a free meal (donations accepted) which included many game dishes (all of which were the first to go) and we supplemented with hamburgers and hot dogs. Our men did all of the cooking and the ladies provided desserts. We did have the event offsite, hoping that would draw more people, as opposed to having it at the church. Praise the Lord we had twenty nine decisions for Christ and two that want to know more. We will work over the upcoming weeks to follow up with those decisions."

Sports evangelism during worldwide sports events

There are times each year when the people of the world turn their attention to major sports event. They are glued to their TV sets during the Olympic Games, World Cup of soccer, The Super Bowl of football, the World Series of baseball, the NBA playoff final games, the Wimbledon tournament of tennis, the US Open of golf, the Stanley Cup of ice hockey, the NASCAR races, and many more. These events are ready made opportunities for Christians to invite their non- Christian friends into their homes or churches to watch these spectacular games, matches and races together. We should offer refreshments and a pleasant atmosphere even if our team is losing. The half time, or the breaks during periods, can become good occasions to ask spiritual questions and to share Jesus Christ with our guests

Sports evangelism camps

Finally, I need to mention an activity that demands a lot of experience, many workers, thorough preparation, and a well executed plan. Before a director of sports ministry decides to organize a camp, he should implement first the less demanding activities like clinics, tournaments and leagues. Camps are popular throughout America especially in summer months when children have prolonged vacation. Camps give churches the longest time with participants who sign up for a whole week. Since most churches cannot provide accommodation, camps should be offered from 9:00am to 12:00pm or from 6:00pm to 9:00pm Monday through Friday. Coaches must balance instruction, practice, and competition with time to rest and to eat snacks. Also, they must not forget to allow sufficient time for prayer, Bible teaching, testimonies, discussions, and the presentation of the Gospel.

Richland Creek Community Church in Wake Forest, North Carolina conducted a sports camp in the summer of 2002 targeting children who didn't go to church in their community. There were too many children who wanted to participate. So the director made a decision to sign up the outsiders in order that they could minister to the unchurched children. Seventeen of those kids made professions of faith and their families began to attend Richland Creek. This is a great example of doing sports evangelism. Our main objective must be outreach.

COMMUNICATING ON THE PLAYING FIELD

In America, we are living in a sports crazy culture. The playing field is wide open to anyone who wants to enter it and participate in it. Knowing about the possible avenues of entering this vast culture is not enough. We have to take the necessary steps to find ourselves in the midst of sports activities that will enable us to communicate with about 95% of Americans and most of the people in the rest of the world. Sports are the common ground that is available for our presence and proclamation.

Oral Roberts founded his university in Tulsa, Oklahoma in 1965. He immediately realized the benefit of sports programs for his school and God's kingdom. He claimed, "Athletics is part of our Christian witness...Nearly every man in America reads the sport pages, and a Christian school cannot ignore these people...Sports are becoming the No. 1 interest of people in America. For us to be relevant, we had to gain the attention of millions of people in a way that they could understand."[8] I played tennis for ORU as I represented the school throughout America. Our team competed against many schools and we had great opportunities to share the gospel of Jesus Christ. We also helped spread the news about a new school when we played in major tournaments.

Newspaper reporters were curious about the relation of sports and a Christian university. They wrote articles about us and some of them included our testimonies about our faith.

Another visionary, Jerry Falwell, initiated sports in his Liberty University. Already in 1970, he explained, "To me, athletics are a way of making a statement. I believe you have a better Christian witness to the youth of the world when you competitively, head-to-head, prove yourself their equal on the playing field."[9] Entering the world of sports demanded a major effort from these universities, but the vision persisted and these institutions are still competing in NCAA. Other Christian organizations focus on sports as a tool to evangelize secular people. They support athletes who want to use their platforms for an ever wider witness for Christ. Some of them are the Fellowship of Christian Athletes, Sports Ambassadors, Athletes in Action, Sports Outreach of America, Pro Athletes Outreach, Church Sports International, and International Sports Federation. Their objective is to bring the gospel to sports minded people everywhere in our world. They are succeeding even in countries that are closed to traditional missions because of their nonthreatening platform of first playing or coaching sports.

The future of the relationship of sports and Christianity

Christians have been pioneering the possibility of a mutual and beneficial relationship with sports especially in the past two hundred years. This is not true about other world religions. Coakley explains, "It seems that certain dimensions of Christian beliefs and meanings can be constructed in ways that fit well with the beliefs and meanings underlying participation and success in organized competitive sports. In fact, it may be that organized competitive sports offer a combination of experiences and meanings that are uniquely compatible with the major characteristics of what sociologists describe as the Protestant Ethic."[10] Most Christians are willing to overlook differences arising from moral and ethical problems in two different worlds. They try to emphasize the positive aspects of sports like spiritual growth through overcoming difficulties, the development of strong character, perseverance to win, building a strong body, and the provision of a common ground to share the Christian faith.

The future of Christianity is guaranteed by the promise of Jesus in Matthew 28:20, "And surely I am with you always, to the very end of the age." And the future of sports seems quite bright, at least for now. Especially power and performance sports will continue to dominate in our culture. They appeal to the athletes who like to prove their superiority by intimidating and defeating their opponents. The fans rejoice and applaud their players when they are winning and they are saddened when they are losing. But fans are forgiving, at least for a short period of time, because they will be back to cheer their warriors again. They are even ready to pay a lot of money to see the battle. They think that their presence brought about the desired win. Then there are the sponsors who want to be associated with winners who help them promote their products. They are helping clubs to continue competing and creating celebrities who are highly marketable. This phenomenon is happening on a world wide scale even in countries that are not as rich as Americans.

We need to mention another model for sports that emphasizes pleasure and participation. These sports are more about personal enjoyment and expression without the burden of having to defeat the opponent. They connect people who want to play for the sake of good health, relieving stress, and the joy of physical activity. Pleasure and participation sports do not generate willing sponsors so the growth will be slow. But with the graying of America, we might see more institutions providing funds, space, and coaching for sports where winning is not everything.

Christians should understand these two models in order to adjust their methodology of penetrating both of them.

Former professional, college, and high school athletes are well equipped to reach out to those who are immersed in power and performance sports. Christians with no competitive background in sports can easily associate with athletes who play sports for the fun of participating in a playful activity. The future of these ministries rests with us Christians. As we represent Christ in the midst of a secular sports culture, we can claim the presence and blessings of God.

Fulfilling Christ's command through sports evangelism

There is no doubt in my mind that our involvement in sports evangelism is a gift of God to us in the 21st century. Jesus is aware of the increasing difficulty we face in order to connect with people who are being influenced by secularization. Our efforts have not been strong enough to slow down the growth of the secular population. We can no longer afford doing ministries that are not effective. We need to proclaim the same gospel and be missional in our approach to non-Christians. Here is the test. Are they going to see us as different from them, yet loving, understanding, and helpful? Are they going to see the reflection of the real Christ in us as we join them in their stadiums, parks, and gymnasiums? Are we convinced that we have something exceptional to offer that cannot be found anywhere else? If we pass this test, we are ready to go out and communicate the Good News of Jesus Christ on the playing fields of the whole world and be winners in the kingdom of God.

APPENDIX ONE

SPORTS EVANGELISM BIBLIOGRAPHY

Barton, George A. *My Lifetime in Sports*. Minneapolis: Olympic Press, 1957.

Ballantine, Peter. *Sport-the Opiate of the People*. Nottingham: Grove Books, 1988.

Baum, Gregory and Coleman, John eds. *Sport*. Edinburgh: T&T Clark, 1989.

Brouwer, Sigmund. *The Edge. Courage and Inspiration from the Ice*. Nashville: J. Countryman, 2000.

Butt, Dorcas Susan. *Psychology of Sport*. New York: Van Nostrand Reinhold, 1987.

Coakley, Jay. *Sport in Society*. Colorado Springs: University of Colorado, 2001.

__________. *Handbook of Sports Studies*. Colorado Springs: University of Colorado, 2000.

Connor, Steve. *Sports Outreach. Principles and Practices for Successful Ministry*. Glasgow: Christian Focus, 2003.

Dayton, Edward R. and Fraser David A. *Planning Strategies for World Evangelization*. Grand Rapids: Eerdmans, 1990.

Dayton, Edward R. and Engstrom, Ted W. *Strategy for Living*. Ventura: Regal Books, 1976.

Garner, John ed. *Recreation and Sports Ministry. Impacting Postmodern Culture*. Nashville: Broadman & Holman, 2003.

Green, Michael. *Evangelism through the Local Church*. Nashville: Nelson, 1992.

Guttman, Allen. *From Ritual to Record: The Nature of Modern Sports*. New York: Columbia, 1978.

Harris, Gerald. *Olympic Heroes. World-Class Athletes Winning at Life*. Nashville: Broadman & Holman, 1996.

Higgs, R. J. *God in the Stadium: Sports and Religion in America*. Lexington: The University of Kentucky Press, 1995.

Hoffman, S. J. *Sport and Religion*. Champaign: Human Kinetics, 1992.

Hubbard, S. *Faith in Sports: Athletes and their Religion on and off the Field*. New York: Doubleday, 1998.

Huizinga, Johan. *Homo Ludens. A Study of the Play Element in Culture*. Boston: Beacon, 1962.

Hunter, George G. *How to Reach Secular People*. Nashville: Abingdon, 1992.

Kellog, Clark. *Heart of a Champion*. Nashville: Broadman & Holman, 2000.

Ladd, Timothy and Mathisen James A. *Mascular Christianity*. Grand Rapids: Baker, 1999.

Mihalich, Joseph C. *Sports and Athletics. Philosophy in Action*. Littlefield: Adams, 1982.

Moltmann, Jurgen. *Theology of Play*. New York: Harper and Row, 1972.

Morrow, Greg and Morrow, Steve. *Recreation: Reaching out, Reaching in, Reaching up*. Nashville: Convention Press, 1986.

Novak, Michael. *The Joy of Sports. End Zones, Bases, Baskets, Balls, and the Consecration of the American Spirit*. New York: Basic Books, 1976.

Oswald, Rodger. *A Theology of Sports Ministry*. Campbell: Church Sports International, 1993.

Peters, George W. *A Biblical Theology of Missions*. Chicago: Moody, 1972.

Simonson, Ted ed. *The Goal and the Glory*. Westwood: Fleming H. Revell, 1962.

Talamini, John T. and Page, Charles. *Sport and Society: An Anthology*. Boston: Little, Brown, 1973

White, John and White, Cindy. *Game Day Glory. Life-Changing Principles for Sport*. Tallmadge:S.D. Meyers, 2006.

APPENDIX TWO

Sports Evangelism Resources

4 Winds Christian Athletics (track & field)
www.4wca.org

Adventures in Missions
www.adventures.org

Ambassadors in Sport
www.aisint.org

Association of Christian Youth Sports
www.acys.org/

Association of Sports and Recreation Ministries
www.csrm.org

Athletes in Action
www.athletesinaction.com

Athletes in Action
www.aia.com/

Athletic Ministries International (Brilla, Spirit Express)
www.athleticministries.org

Baptist Standard (Texas Baptist Newsjournal)
www.baptiststandard.com

Baseball Chapel
www.baseballchapel.org

Baseball Country
www.baseballcountry.com

Baseball Missions
www.upi.org

Baseball without Borders
www.baseballwithoutborders.com

Basketball Missions
www.nrbasketball.org

Belhaven College -sports ministry courses
www.belhaven.edu/academics/SportsMinistry

Beyond Soccer
www.beyondsoccer.org/about.asp

Big Life Sports
www.biglifesports.org

BMX and MotoX
www.riders4christ.com/

BP Sports
www.bpsports.net

Breakaway Outreach
www.jimmylarche.com

Campus Crusade for Christ
www.ccci.org

Catholic Athletes for Christ
www.catholicathletesforchrist.org

Champions for Christ
www.championsfc.com

Chang Family Foundation -Christian Sports League
www.mchang.com/cff/sportsleague.html

Charlotte Eagles Soccer
www.charlotteeagles.com

Chinese Christian Union Sports
www.ccusports.com/

Christian Bowhunters of America
www.christianbowhunters.org

Christian Canadian Sports Magazine
www.christiansportsmag.com/

Christian Climbers
www.srcfc.org

Christian Sports Association
www.csa-sports.org/

Christian Sports International
www.csikids.org/pages/

Christian Sports Minute
www.christiansportsminute.com

Christian Surfers of Australia
www.christiansurfers.org.au

Christian Taekwondo Fellowship
www.christiantaekwondofellowship.com/
Christian Team Ministries
www.christianteam.org

Christian Triathlons
www.ictrinet.com/

Christians in Sport
www.christiansinsport.org.uk

Christian-Sports
www.christian-sports.com/html/Home.htm

Church Sports International
www.churchsports.org

Church Sports Outreach
www.churchsportsoutreach.org

College Golf Fellowship
www.cgfonline.org/

Cowboys for Christ
www.cowboysforchrist.net

Cross Training (Basketball Camps)
www.crosstrainingcamp.com

Crosspoint sports camps
www.lifeway.com/crosspoint

Crosswalk
www.crosswalk.com

Decision Magazine
www.billygraham.org/DMag_article_index.asp

Directory - Sports Resources
www.missionresources.com/sportsoutreach.html

EvangeSport
www.worldmethodist.org/evangesport.
htm

Extreme Sports
www.radicalriders.com/

Extreme Sports Missions
www.extremesportsmissions.com

Faith and Fitness Magazine
www.faithandfitness.net

FCA Golf
www.fcagolf.org

FCA Lacrosse
www.fcalax.org

Fellowship of Christian Anglers
www.focas.org/

Fellowship of Christian Athletes
www.fca.org

Fellowship of Christian Athletes-North Carolina
www.webfca.com/northcarolina

Fields of Faith (Student-Led Event)
www.fieldsoffaith.com/

Game Changers
www.gamechangers.org/

Global Youth Baseball
www.baseballwithoutborders.com

Good News & Crossway (books, tracts)
www.gnpcb.org

Gospel Communications
www.gospel.com

HIS (Harvesters in Sport) Ministries
www.harvestersinsport.co.zw/

Hockey Ministries International
www.hockeyministries.org

Hoops of Hope
www.hoops.org

Houghton College Sports Ministry Webpage
www.houghton.edu

Infinity Sports
www.infinitysports.com

International Sports Evangelists
www.internationalsportsevangelists.org/

International Sports Federation
www.sportsmissions.com

International Sports Federation
www.teamisf.com

Intervarsity Christian Fellowship
www.ivcf.org
JEMS Sports and Recreation Ministry
www.jems.org/sports

Lifeway
www.lifeway.com

Links Players International
www.linksplayers.com/

Livin It
www.livinit.com

Malone College Sports Ministry Webpage
www.malone.edu/2202

Meeting places for Christian Athletes
http://christianath.meetup.com

Mennonite Sports Organization
www.mennonitesports.org/

Ministry to Pro Athletes
www.pao.org

Missionary Athletes International (Soccer)
www.maisoccer.com

Motor Racing Outreach
www.go2mro.com

Motorsports Evangelism
www.teamjesus.org

Motorsports Ministries
www.motorsportsministries.org/

National Christian College Athletic Association
www.thenccaa.org/

North American Mission Board (NAMB)
www.namb.net

On Mission (magazine)
www.onmission.com

Operation Mobilization
www.om.org

Push the Rock
www.pushtherock.org

Run To Win Outreach
www.runtowin.faithsite.com/

Score Chaplaincy (United Kingdom)
www.scorechaplaincy.org.uk

Score International
www.scoreinternational.org

Scripture Union Sportz
www.susportz.org

Sharing the Victory—Faith and Sport (FCA)
www.sharingthevictory.org/

Sports Ambassadors
www.gospelcom.net/oci/sa/sports.htm

Sports Ambassadors
www.onechallenge.org
Sports and Rec Plus
www.sportsrecplus.org

Sports Chaplains
www.sportschaplains.org/

Sports Crusaders
www.sportscrusaders.org

Sports Evangelism & Mission
www.sportevangelism.com

Sports Impact
www.sportsimpact.org.au

Sports Life - Sierra Leone
www.sportslife-sl.info/about.htm

Sports Link (Operation Mobilization)
www.go2sportslink.org

Sports Ministry Magazine
www.sportsspectrum.com

Sports Ministry Outreach
www.sportsoutreach.org

Sports Outreach Institute
www.sportsoutreachinstitute.org/wp/

Sports Outreach International
www.sportsoutreach.com

Sports Outreach Los Angeles
www.sportsoutreachla.org
Sports Related Gospel Tracts
www.crossway.org/catalog/sports/tracts

Sports Spectrum Radio
www.rbc.org/radio-tv/sports-spectrum/home.aspx

Sports Witnesses (Dutch site)
www.sportswitnesses.nl

Sports World Camp
www.sportsworldcamp.org

SRS (German site)
www.srsonline.de

Tennis Ministry International
www.tennisministry.org

The Beach Team
www.thebeachteam.org

The Chang Family Foundation
www.mchang.com

The Goal
www.thegoal.com

To the Next Level
www.tothenextlevel.org

Tracts - Search by Category: Sports
www.atstracts.org/index.php

Unlimited Potential
www.upi.org

Upward Sports
www.upward.org
UW (Uncharted Waters) Sports Ministry
www.uwsportsministry.org/

Vapor Sports Ministries
www.vaporsports.org/

Wilderness Ministry Institute
www.wildernessministry.org/

World Sports Ministries
www.worldsportministries.com

World Sports Ministry
www.infinitysports.com

Youth Coaching Information
www.y-coach.com/

Youth with a Mission
www.ywam.com

NOTES

Chapter One

[1] This quote is taken from *Glorious Hope*. Published by The Czechoslovak Baptist Convention, March 2001, 45.
[2] Jurgen Moltmann, *Theology of Play* (New York: Harper & Row, 1971), 19
[3] Allen Guttmann. *From Ritual to Record. The Nature of modern Sports* (New York: Columbia University, 1978), 3.
[4] Peter Ballantine. *Sport – The Opiate of the People* (Nottingham: Grove Books, 988), 3.
[5] Gregory Baum and John Coleman, *Concilium. Religion in the Eighties: Sport (* Edinburgh: T&T Clark, 1989), 93.
[6] Thomas Hughes, *Tom Brown at Oxford (*London: Macmillan, 1861), 83
[7] Tony Ladd and James A. Mathisen, *Muscular Christianity. Evangelical Protestants and the Development of American Sport (*Grand Rapids: Baker, 1999), 16.
[8] Jay Coakley, *Sports in Society. Issues and Controversies* (New York: McGraw Hill, 2004), 528-29.
[9] Bob Briner, *Roaring Lambs* (Grand Rapids: Zondervan, 1993), 31.
[10] John and Cindy White. *Game Day Glory* (Tallmadge: S. D. Meyers, 2006), 122.
[11] Coakley, 532.
[12] Harvey Cox, *The Secular City* (Middlesex: Penguin, 1968), 15.
[13] Thomas Oden, *Two Worlds* (Downers Grove: Inter Varsity, 1992), 33-36.

Chapter Two

Clark Kellogg, *Heart of a Champion* (Nashville: Broadman & Holman, 2001), 9.
[2] http://www.upward.org/about.aspx
[3] Lewis A Drummond, *The Word of the Cross* (Nashville: Broadman and Holman, 1992), 9.
[4] Wilfrid J. Harrington, *The Path of Biblical Theology* (Dublin: Gill and Macmillan, 1973), 350.
[5] Brevard S. Childs, *Biblical Theology in Crisis* (Philadelphia: Westminster, 1976), 99.
[6]Robert J. Hicks, *God in the Stadium. Sports and Religion in America* (Lexinngton: The University Press of Kentucky, 1995), 1.
[7] Ibid., 14

Chapter Three

[1] C. E. Autrey, *The Theology of Evangelism* (Nashville: Broadman and Holman, 1966), 22.
[2] Drummond, *The Word of the Cross,* 98.
[3] Milliard J. Erickson, *Christian Theology* (Grand Rapids: Baker, 1985), 346.
[4] C.F. Keil and F. Delitzsch, *Commentary on the Old Testament in Ten Volumes* (Grand Rapids: Michigan, 1973), 102.
[5] Drummond, *The Word of the Cross,* 234.
[6]Nels Ferre, *The Christian Understanding of God* (New York: Harper & Row, 1951), 237.
[7] Erickson, *Christian Theology,* 835.
[8] Leighton Ford, *The Christian* Persuader (New York: Harper & Row, 1966), 119.
[9] Ibid., 16.
[10] Ibid., 17.
[11] Ibid., 23-25.
[12] George W. Peters, *A Biblical Theology of Missions* (Chicago: Moody, 1972), 46.
[13] Drummond, *The Word of the Cross,* 143.
[14] P. T. Forsyth, *The Cruciality of the Cross* (London: Hodder & Stoughton, 1909), 44.
[15] Frederick Dale Brunner, *A Theology of the Holy Spirit* (Grand Rapids: Eerdmans, 1970), 201.

[16] Afapetition@afa.net from June 21, 2006.
[17] Paige Patterson, *The Troubled Triumphant Church* (Nashville: Nelson, 1983), 148-149.
[18] Ibid., 150.
[19] Alexander Maclaren, *Expositions of Holy Scripture. Corinthians.* Grand Rapids: Baker, 1982), 142.

Chapter Four

[1] Dallas, Willard, *The Spirit of the Disciplines* (San Francisco: Harper Collins, 1990), 29-30.
[2] Ibid., 31.
[3] David L. Goetz, "The Riddle of Our Postmodern Culture: What is Postmodernism? Should we Even Care?" *Leadership,* Winter 1997, 53.
[4] Will McRaney, *The art of Personal Evangelism* (Nashville: B&H, 2003), 127-128.
[5] Ibid., 128-129
[6] Dietrich Bonhoeffer, *The Cost of Discipleship* (New York: Macmillan, 1972), 54.
[7] Ibid., 32.
[8] Willard, 68.
[9] Ibid., 68.
[10] Ibid., 158.
[11] Richard Foster, *Celebration of Discipline. The Path to Spiritual Growth* (San Francisco: Harper, 1988), v.
[12] Ibid., 157.
[13] Donald S. Whitney, *Spiritual Disciplines for the Christian Life* (Colorado Springs: NavPress, 1991), 107.
[14] Francis de Sales, *Introduction to the Devout Life (*Garden City: Doubleday, 1957), 43-44.
[15] Millard Erickson, *Truth or Consequences. The Promise and Perils of Postmodernism* (Downers Grove: InterVarsity, 2001), 313.
[16] James Engel & William Dyrness, *Changing the Mind of Missions. Where Have We Gone Wrong?* (Downers Grove: InterVarsity, 2000), 101.
[17] Rebecca Manley Pippert, *Out of the Salt Shaker and into the World* (Downers Grove: InterVarsity,
1999), 142-145.
[18] Ibid., 143.

[19] Paul Little, *How to Give Away your Faith* (Downers Grove: InterVarsity, 1988), 63-64.
[20] Michael Green, *Evangelism through the Local Church* (Nashville: Thomas Nelson, 1992), 35-37.
[21] Ibid., 37.
[22] Karl Menninger, *Whatever Became of Sin* (New York: Bantam, 1978), 22.
[23] Ibid., 23.
[24] Ibid., 52.
[25] Ibid., 264
[26] Robert Webber, *Common Roots* (Grand Rapids: Zondervan, 1978), 165.
[27] Alvin Reid, *Introduction to Evangelism* (Nashville: Broadman & Holman, 1998), 105.
[28] William McRaney, *The Art of Personal Evangelism* (Nashville: Broadman &Holman, 2003), 191.
[29] William Fay and Ralph Hodge, *Share Jesus Without Fear* (Nashville: LifeWay, 1997), 46-48.
[30] McRainey, *The Art of Personal Evangelism*, 193.

Chapter Five

Clark, Kellogg. *Heart of a Champion* (Nashville: Broadman & Holman, 2001), 218-219.
[2] Johan, Huizinga. *Homo Ludens. A Study of the Play Element in Culture* (Boston: The Beacon, 1950), 1.
[3] Ibid., 5.
[4] Ibid., 199.
[5] Edward, Dayton and David A. Fraser. *Planning Strategies for World Evangelization* (Grand Rapids: Eerdmanns, 1990), 287.
[6] John, Garner. *Recreation and Sports Ministry* (Nashville: Broadman & Holman, 2003), 153.
[7] Ibid., 153.
[8] Alan, Hirsch. *The Forgotten Ways* (Grand Rapids: Brazos, 2006), 36.
[9] John T. Sizemore. *The Ministry of Religious Education* (Nashville: Broadman), 72.
[10] George, Peters. *A Biblical Theology of Missions* (Chicago: Moody, 1972), 187.
[11] Dayton, 13.

[12] Ibid., 15.
[13] Ibid., 211-212.
[14] Aubrey, Malphurs. *Advanced Strategic Planning* (Grand Rapids: Baker, 2005), 10-11.
[15] Ibid., 11-12.
[16] Ibid., 26.
[17] Dayton, 174.
[18] Robert E. Coleman. *The Master Plan of Evangelism* (Grand Rapids: Baker), 27.
[19] Ibid., 42.
[20] Ibid., 65.
[21] Ibid., 95.
[22] Dayton, 287.
[23] A. H. Maslow. *Motivation and Personality* (New York: Harper, 1954), 80-92.
[24] Ibid., 91- 92.
[25] George G. Hunter. *How to Reach Secular People* (Nashville: Abingdon, 1992), 26-29.
[26] Ibid., 35-36.

Chapter Six

[1] Hirsch, 128.
[2] Hunter, 119.
[3] Henry T. Blackaby and Claude King. *Experiencing God. Knowing and Doing the Will of God* (Nashville: The Sunday School Board of the SBC, 1990), 15.
[4] Tim Downs. *Finding Common Ground* (Chicago: Moody, 1999), 178-79.
[5] Aubrey Malphurs. *Planting Growing Churches for the 21st Century* (Grand Rapids: Baker, 1998), 35.
[6] Hirsch, 145.
[7] Dayton, 294.
[8] Coakley, 470.
[9] Ibid., 470.
[10] Ibid., 485.

You can contact Dr. Josef Solc for further information and speaking engagements at jsolc@sebts.edu.

You can also check his webpage: www.jsev.org